Spelling
Workout

Phillip K. Trocki

MODERN CURRICULUM PRESS

COVER DESIGN: Pronk & Associates

ILLUSTRATIONS: Jim Steck

PHOTOGRAPHS: All photos © Pearson Learning unless otherwise noted.

Cover: *t.r.*, *m.l.* Artbase Inc., *b.r.* Tim Davis/Stone.
5: Gavriel Jecan/Stone. 8: Ben Osborne/Stone. 9: Dave King/Dorling Kindersley. 12: Steve Bronstein/The Image Bank. 13: © Peter David/Photo Researchers, Inc. 16: © Andrew J. Martinez/Photo Researchers, Inc. 20: SuperStock, Inc. 21: Tom Haseltine/FPG International. 29: Travis Anderson/Courtesy Schmitt Music Co. 33, 36: David Young-Wolff/PhotoEdit. 37: Myrleen Ferguson Cate/PhotoEdit. 40: Pearson Education/PH College. 41: Hulton Getty/Liaison International. 45: © Ken M. Highfill/Photo Researchers, Inc. 48: Steve Kaufman/Peter Arnold, Inc. 51: Lori Adamski Peek/Stone. 53: Thomas Del Brase/Stone. 55: Tom Vezo/Peter Arnold, Inc. 61: Corbis. 64: © Porterfield/Chickering/Photo Researchers, Inc. 65: Neil Beer/PhotoDisc, Inc. 68: Jim Cummins/FPG International. 69: Yann Arthus-Bertrand/Corbis. 72: José L. Pelaez/Corbis Stock Market. 77: Michael Boys/Corbis. 80: Patrick Johns/Corbis 81: Janice L. Edwards for the National Hollerin' Contest. 84: Hulton Getty/Liaison International. 85: Frank Lan Picture Agency/Corbis. 88: Steve Kaufman/Corbis. 92: Hulton-Deutsch Collection/Corbis. 93: Ecoscene/Corbis. 96: Bettmann/Corbis. 98: Tracy Morgan/Dorling Kindersley. 101: AFP/Corbis. 104: Allsport Photography. 105: Lawrence Migdale/Stone. 108: Esbin/Anderson/Omni-Photo Communications, Inc. 109: Felicia Martinez/PhotoEdit. 112: Mitch Hrdlicka/PhotoDisc, Inc. 113: Ivan Polunin/Bruce Coleman Inc. 116: E.R. Degginger/Bruce Coleman Inc. 119: heads Pearson Education/PH College, tails Bettmann/Corbis. 122: PhotoDisc, Inc. 125: Bob Krist/Corbis. 128: James Lemass/Index Stock Imagery/PictureQuest. 129: Photodisc Imaging/PhotoDisc, Inc. 132: Tony Freeman/PhotoEdit. 133: Bill Ross/Corbis. 136: AFL-CIO. 137: Kennan Ward/Corbis Stock Market. 144: Paul A. Souders/Corbis.

Acknowledgments

ZB Font Method Copyright © 1996 Zaner-Bloser.

Some content in this product is based upon *Webster's New World Dictionary for Young Adults*. © 2001 Hungry Minds, Inc. All rights reserved. Webster's New World is a trademark or registered trademark of Hungry Minds, Inc.

NOTE: Every effort has been made to locate the copyright owner of material reprinted in this book. Omissions brought to our attention will be corrected in subsequent editions.

ISBN 0-7652-2482-8

Printed in the United States of America
11 12 13 14 15   12 11 10 09 08

Modern
Curriculum
Press

Pearson Learning Group

1-800-321-3106
www.pearsonlearning.com

Table of Contents

Learning to Spell a Word

1. Say the word.
   Look at the word and say the letters.

2. Write the word with your finger.

3. Close your eyes and think of the word.

4. Cover the word and write it on paper.

5. Check your spelling.

Keeping a Spelling Notebook

A spelling notebook will help you when you write.
Write the words you're having trouble with on a separate
sheet of paper or in the **Spelling Notebook**
at the back of the book.

Lesson 1

Spelling Words in Action

What is almost nine-feet tall and lays eggs?

A Very Big Bird

What has feathers, runs **fast**, and is taller than the tallest basketball player? It's the biggest **bird** in the world, the ostrich. This giant fowl can grow to be almost **nine**-feet tall.

Some people think that ostriches bury their heads in the sand. They believe that ostriches are hiding from their enemies. The ostrich has no reason to hide from anything. An ostrich can run up to 40 miles an hour! That's faster than most of its enemies. These huge birds can weigh over 350 pounds. One kick from an ostrich could **kill** a **person**. The ostrich does have one small problem. Unlike most other birds, it **cannot** fly!

Ostrich hens lay their eggs in holes in the ground. One **egg** is often larger than a softball. If you wanted to boil an ostrich egg, you'd need plenty of **water**. When it was cooked, you could use it to make egg salad. You'd have enough to make as many as 20 sandwiches! That's **quite** a meal!

Say the words in dark print. What consonant sounds do you hear?

Spelling Practice

TIP

The alphabet has two kinds of letters. The **vowels** are **a, e, i, o, u,** and sometimes **y.** All the other letters are **consonants.** Read the **list words.** Some words have one syllable, as in bird. Some words have more than one syllable as in forest. Notice that each syllable has its own vowel sound.

LIST WORDS

1. fast   *fast*
2. bird   *bird*
3. nine   *nine*
4. life   *life*
5. since   *since*
6. kill   *kill*
7. cannot   *cannot*
8. egg   *egg*
9. water   *water*
10. mark   *mark*
11. person   *person*
12. quite   *quite*
13. beside   *beside*
14. sister   *sister*
15. forest   *forest*

Syllables

Write the **list words** that have one syllable.

1. _____
2. _____
3. _____
4. _____
5. _____
6. _____
7. _____
8. _____
9. _____

Write the **list words** that have two syllables.

10. _____
11. _____
12. _____
13. _____
14. _____
15. _____

Puzzle

Write the **list word** whose meaning matches each clue.
Read down the shaded boxes to answer the riddle.

1. not slow

2. next to

3. a girl related to other children in her family

4. this has a yolk and a shell

5. entirely

6. a colorless liquid

7. a human being

8. the number after eight

9. many trees

What kind of sound does a three-hundred-pound bird make?

Answer: __ __ __ __ __ __ __ __ __ __

Rhyming Words

Write the **list word** that rhymes with each word.

1. wife _____

2. prince _____

3. drill _____

4. third _____

5. spark _____

6. white _____

7. pine _____

8. mister _____

9. ride _____

10. beg _____

Spelling and Writing

Proofreading

Each sentence below has two mistakes. Use the proofreading marks to fix the mistakes. Write the misspelled **list words** correctly on the lines.

1. The hummingbird is the berd with the smallest eeg.

1. _____

   _____

2. a duck has feet shaped like paddles so it can swim in the watter.

2. _____

3. Penguins canot fly, but they can swim faste.

3. _____

   _____

4. An eagle lives in the african rain forrest.

4. _____

Writing a Descriptive Paragraph

Birds come in many colors, shapes, and sizes. Write a description of one or more birds you have seen or know about. Include details, such as what they look and sound like. Use as many **list words** as you can. Be sure to proofread your description. Fix any mistakes.

_____

_____

_____

_____

_____

_____

BONUS WORDS

carpet

shirt

sidewalk

mile

canvas

Spelling Words in Action

How does the magic ladybug move?

Presto!

The magician stands before the crowd. He holds up a plain sheet of paper. He shows the crowd that there's nothing on either side. He **places** a paper ladybug onto the page. Presto! It sticks. Next, he says, "Ladybug, ladybug, turn around." Then, as the **faces** in the crowd look on, the bug begins to move. He makes the paper bug **climb** up and down and all around the page. It's **magic**!

Here's how you can do the trick, too. First, draw a **giant** ladybug, then cut it out. Tape a large paper clip onto the back of the picture. Then, hide a small magnet in your hand. Hold the paper with the magnet hidden in your hand. **Pick** up the bug, but be sure not to show the paper clip. **Once** you have your magnet in place behind the paper, the ladybug will stick. **Give** the magnet a push and the ladybug will move. No one will know how you did it.

Look back at the words in dark print. Say each word. What two sounds does the c make? What two sounds does the g make?

Spelling Practice

LIST WORDS

1.	ice	*ice*
2.	pick	*pick*
3.	gone	*gone*
4.	case	*case*
5.	faces	*faces*
6.	cage	*cage*
7.	magic	*magic*
8.	age	*age*
9.	wagon	*wagon*
10.	give	*give*
11.	giant	*giant*
12.	once	*once*
13.	danger	*danger*
14.	places	*places*
15.	climb	*climb*

Sounds of <u>c</u> and <u>g</u>

Write the **list word** that has a hard or soft **c** under the correct heading. One word has both the soft **g** and the hard **c**.

hard **c** as in <u>car</u>	soft **c** as in <u>city</u>
1. _____	6. _____
2. _____	7. _____
3. _____	8. _____
4. _____	9. _____
5. _____	

Write the **list word** that has a hard or soft **g** under the correct heading.

soft **g** as in <u>page</u>	hard **g** as in <u>game</u>
10. _____	15. _____
11. _____	16. _____
12. _____	17. _____
13. _____	
14. _____	

Puzzle

Write a **list word** to complete each sentence. Then, read down the shaded boxes to answer the riddle.

1. It takes strong legs to _____ a mountain.

2. Tom went to many _____ on his trip.

3. The sign read, " _____! Ice on the Road!"

4. Jack climbed the beanstalk and met a _____.

5. The bottles of juice came in a cardboard _____.

Riddle: What would you need to take an elephant for a ride on your bike?

Answer: ___ ___ ___ ___ ___

Vocabulary

Write the **list word** that matches each clue.

1. It can carry a heavy load. _____

2. A pet bird may live in this. _____

3. It will make your drink cold. _____

4. Tales may start " _____ upon a time." _____

5. He was here, but now he's _____. _____

6. These have eyes and mouths. _____

7. This means the opposite of take. _____

8. This means choose. _____

9. This means how old a person is. _____

10. Presto! A rabbit's in my hat! _____

Spelling and Writing

Proofreading

Each sentence below has two mistakes. Use the proofreading marks to fix the mistakes. Write the misspelled **list words** correctly on the lines.

1. the magician asks Roy to pik a card.

2. He plases Roy's card in a large hat and waves a majic wand.

3. Now he will giv the jiant hat a tap.

4. suddenly, the card is gon!

5. do you see the surprise on all the fases?

1. _____

2. _____

   _____

3. _____

   _____

4. _____

5. _____

Writing Directions

What magic tricks have you seen? Maybe you know how to do a magic trick yourself. Use the **list words** to write directions telling how it's done. Be sure to proofread your work. Fix any mistakes.

_____

_____

_____

_____

_____

BONUS WORDS

cargo

garage

glisten

pack

exercise

Spelling Words in Action

Where does the anglerfish keep its fishing line?

Something Fishy

An "angler" is a person who fishes with a hook and a line. Have you ever heard of an anglerfish? If you think it's a fish that goes fishing, you're close. It **does** go fishing—with its own line and bait!

The deep-sea anglerfish does not "fish" in the usual way. It does not hang its line down into the water. It does its fishing from the **bottom** of the ocean. The anglerfish stays deep **under** the water. Like a **rock** on the ocean floor, it does not move. It does look up because **its** eyes are toward the top of its head. Its fishing lines are on top of its head, too! These float up through the water. When fish swim **past**, they think they see worms. The fish come closer. The anglerfish does not need a hook to catch **them**. When the fish swim up to eat the "worms," the anglerfish will just **gobble** them up.

Say each word in dark print. What vowel sounds do you hear?

Spelling Practice

LIST WORDS

1. little *little*
2. its *its*
3. under *under*
4. rock *rock*
5. dead *dead*
6. past *past*
7. them *them*
8. collar *collar*
9. dug *dug*
10. does *does*
11. gobble *gobble*
12. bottom *bottom*
13. level *level*
14. felt *felt*
15. next *next*

Syllables

Write the **list words** that have one syllable.

1. _____
2. _____
3. _____
4. _____
5. _____
6. _____
7. _____
8. _____
9. _____

Write the **list words** that have two syllables.

10. _____
11. _____
12. _____
13. _____
14. _____
15. _____

Missing Words

Write a **list word** to complete each sentence.

1. The necktie fits under the shirt's _____.

2. You can find apples on the ground _____ the branches of the tree.

3. There is more jam left at the _____ of the jar.

4. Be sure not to _____ up all of the fruit.

5. This ground was once _____ and very flat.

6. Our dog _____ a huge hole in the backyard.

7. What _____ six plus seven equal?

Puzzle

Unscramble the letters to spell **list words**. Print one letter in each box. Then, read down the shaded boxes to answer the riddle.

1. sit

2. xent

3. dade

4. ckor

5. telf

6. tillte

7. stap

8. mhet

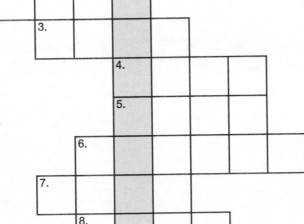

Riddle: What is the most famous fish of all?

Answer: a __ __ __ __ __ __ __ __

Spelling and Writing

Proofreading

Each sentence below has two mistakes. Use the proofreading marks to fix the mistakes. Write the misspelled **list words** correctly on the lines.

1. A flounder fish lives on the ocean bottum

2. It dus look strange because both itz eyes are on the same side of its head.

3. The flat flounder lies levil with the sand

4. It lies uhnder sand that it has duge up.

5. Flounders can be colored like a rok on top

6. People like thim because they are tasty

Proofreading Marks

⊙ add period

◯ spelling mistake

1. _____

2. _____

_____

3. _____

4. _____

_____

5. _____

6. _____

Writing a Poem

Have you ever seen a strange fish, bug, or other animal? Write a poem telling about a real animal or a made-up one. Use as many **list words** as you can. Be sure to proofread your poem. Fix any mistakes.

_____

_____

_____

_____

BONUS WORDS

tender

lack

humble

chop

instead

Spelling Words in Action

What kind of jam won't spread on bread?

A Squiggly Tale

Last week, the Landview Police Department got a call from a Mrs. Sadie Rose who said that there was a huge pig causing a traffic jam on the **main** road through town.

A police unit, with siren wailing, drove to the scene. When they arrived, they indeed found a pig driving down the middle of the street. An officer asked what was the problem.

"Don't **blame** me," said the pig. "None of this is my fault."

"Well, what are you doing here?" asked the officer.

"I'm taking my **daily** drive," the pig tried to **explain**. "I'm on my way to market."

"You can't just drive down the middle of the road," replied the officer. "It's not **safe**," If you don't move, I'm going to have to take you to **jail**."

"I have every right to be here," explained the pig. "I'm a road hog!"

Say each word in dark print in the selection. What vowel sound do you hear in each word?

17

A long vowel sound often has the same sound as its letter name, but it can be spelled in different ways. The long **a** sound can be spelled **a_e**, as in safe and tale. It can also be spelled **ai** as in main and jail.

Spelling Practice

LIST WORDS

1. main	*main*	
2. daily	*daily*	
3. safe	*safe*	
4. jail	*jail*	
5. tale	*tale*	
6. blame	*blame*	
7. explain	*explain*	
8. awake	*awake*	
9. mail	*mail*	
10. raise	*raise*	
11. paid	*paid*	
12. paint	*paint*	
13. baked	*baked*	
14. claim	*claim*	
15. train	*train*	

Long-Vowel Sound a

Write each **list word** under the correct heading.

long **a** spelled **ai**

1. _____

2. _____

3. _____

4. _____

5. _____

6. _____

7. _____

8. _____

9. _____

10. _____

long **a** spelled **a_e**

11. _____

12. _____

13. _____

14. _____

15. _____

Missing Words

Write a **list word** to complete each sentence.

1. Pleasant Street is the _____ road through town.

2. We _____ three dollars for all of the vegetables.

3. The police placed the thief in _____.

4. You can _____ the letter at the post office.

5. The contest winner can _____ the prize at the office.

6. She wanted to _____ the wagon bright red.

7. The potatoes were _____ in a very hot oven.

8. The teacher will _____ how to answer the questions.

9. It is not _____ to cross the street without looking.

10. Because I couldn't sleep, I was _____ most of the night.

Puzzle

Write the **list word** whose meaning matches each clue.

ACROSS
   4. to lift up
   6. to tell about
   7. runs on tracks
   8. to name the cause
      of something
   9. every day

DOWN
   1. a story
   2. not asleep
   3. a liquid covering
   5. cooked in an oven

Spelling and Writing

Proofreading

Proofreading Marks

⬭ spelling mistake

≡ capital letter

Each sentence below has two mistakes. Use the proofreading marks to fix the mistakes. Write the misspelled **list words** correctly on the lines.

1. don't blaim me if you miss the game.

1. _____

2. i usually take a daley walk along the shore.

2. _____

3. please explane why you came to class late.

3. _____

4. she is usually awaik before seven in the morning.

4. _____

5. the trane will leave at two in the afternoon.

5. _____

Writing a Story

Use the **list words** to write a believe-it-or-not tale like the one about the road hog. Include dialogue between the characters. Be sure to proofread your work. Fix any mistakes.

_____

_____

_____

_____

_____

BONUS WORDS

skated

brave

grapes

vases

basic

Spelling Words in Action

How much did the "fat cat" weigh?

Cat Tales

Did you know that there are about 60 million cats in North America? A few are famous. You may have seen them on television or in cartoons. Here are a few felines who are not so famous.

The prize for **size** goes to a cat in Australia. Most cats weigh about ten pounds. This "fat cat" weighed over 46 pounds. That's almost as heavy as **five** bowling balls! While he was **alive**, "fat cat" should have watched his **diet**.

Speaking of eating, most cats **grind** up a mouse or two during their lives. The prize for "mouser" goes to Towser. He lived **inside** a factory in England. He caught almost 29,000 mice.

Finally, the prize for "richest cat" is shared by two cool California cats. When their owner died, he left them all his money. It came to over $400,000. Now that's a lot of cat chow!

Say each word in dark print in the selection. Listen for the long i sound. What do you notice about the ways the long i is spelled?

21

TIP

Words with long **i** sounds can have different spelling patterns.

The long **i** in <u>size</u> is spelled **i_e**.

The long **i** in <u>pies</u> is spelled **ie**.

The long **i** in <u>dial</u> is spelled **ia**.

The long **i** in <u>pint</u> is spelled **i_ _**.

LIST WORDS

1. alive   *alive*
2. grind   *grind*
3. pint   *pint*
4. drive   *drive*
5. diet   *diet*
6. size   *size*
7. rise   *rise*
8. died   *died*
9. tried   *tried*
10. dial   *dial*
11. five   *five*
12. pies   *pies*
13. inside   *inside*
14. cried   *cried*
15. island   *island*

Spelling Practice

Long-Vowel Sound i

Write each **list word** under the correct heading.

long i spelled ie

1. _____
2. _____
3. _____
4. _____
5. _____

long i spelled ia

6. _____

long i spelled i_ _

7. _____
8. _____
9. _____

long i spelled i_e

10. _____
11. _____
12. _____
13. _____
14. _____
15. _____

Vocabulary

Write the **list word** that matches each clue. Then, use the number code to answer the riddle. Find the letter with the number 1 below it. Write that letter on the line with the number 1 below it. Continue with the other numbers.

1. foods you usually eat ___ ___ ___ ___
 3

2. to crush into bits ___ ___ ___ ___ ___
 4

3. living ___ ___ ___ ___ ___
 2

4. yelled out ___ ___ ___ ___ ___
 1

5. how large or small something is ___ ___ ___ ___
 5

6. fruit-filled pastries ___ ___ ___ ___
 6

Riddle: What is a cat's favorite bite? **Answer:** ___ ___ ___ ___ ___ ___
 1 2 3 4 5 6

Alphabetical Order

All words in a dictionary are listed in **alphabetical order**. Write the **list words** from the box in alphabetical order. Follow these rules:

1. If the first letter of two words is the same, then use the second letter.
2. If the first two letters are the same, then use the third letter.

five	tried	dial	died
island	inside	drive	pint

1. _____   5. _____

2. _____   6. _____

3. _____   7. _____

4. _____   8. _____

Spelling and Writing

Proofreading

Each sentence below has two mistakes. Use the proofreading marks to fix the mistakes. Write the misspelled **list words** correctly on the lines.

1. My cat has used fiive of his nine lives

1. _____

2. Once he tride to dile the telephone.

2. _____

_____

3. When I left the house he meowed and cride

3. _____

4. He ate two of my mother's apple pize and drank a pinte of milk.

4. _____

_____

5. Sometimes I think he will drieve me crazy

5. _____

Writing a Descriptive Paragraph

Think of a cat you have seen in real life or on television that did something silly. Write a description of the cat and what it did. Use as many **list words** as you can. Be sure to proofread you work. Fix any mistakes.

BONUS WORDS

bind

diamond

divide

surprise

fries

_____

_____

_____

_____

_____

In lessons 1 through 5, you learned how to spell words with consonants, including hard and soft **c** and **g**. You also learned to spell words with the short vowels and the long vowels **a** and **i**.

Check Your Spelling Notebook

Look at the words in your spelling notebook. Which words in lessons 1 through 5 did you have the most trouble with? Write them here.

_____

_____

Practice writing your troublesome words with a partner. Take turns writing each word as the other slowly spells it aloud.

Lesson 1

 There are two kinds of letters in the alphabet. The **vowels** are **a, e, i, o, u**, and sometimes **y**. All the other letters are **consonants**.

Each riddle has an answer with rhyming words in it. Write a **list word** to finish each answer. One word will not be used.

List Words

bird
sister
quite
water
nine
mark
fast

1. What color is paper?

_____ white

2. Where is that name?

on line _____

3. What is an ink blot?

a dark _____

4. What is a quick boom?

a _____ blast

5. What is next to the second hen?

a third _____

6. How did Mom greet a family member? kissed

her _____

Listen for the hard and soft sounds of the letters **c** and **g**, as in <u>case</u>, <u>ice</u>, <u>age</u>, and <u>gone</u>.

List Words

cage
give
climb
once
wagon
giant
danger

Write the **list word** that goes with each clue. One word will not be used.

1. has wheels _____

2. pet bird's house _____

3. threat _____

4. hand to someone _____

5. only one time _____

6. huge _____

 Short-vowel sounds are often spelled with just one vowel, as in <u>dug</u>. Notice the different spellings of the short-vowel sounds in <u>dead</u> and <u>does</u>.

List Words

under
collar
does
dead
bottom
level

Write the **list words** in alphabetical order.

1. _____

2. _____

3. _____

4. _____

5. _____

6. _____

The long-vowel sound often has the same sound as its letter name. The long **a** sound can be spelled **a_e** as in safe and **ai** as in main.

List Words

tale
paid
mail
baked
safe
main
train
blame

Write each **list word** under the correct heading.

long **a** spelled **ai**

1. _____

2. _____

3. _____

4. _____

long **a** spelled **a_e**

5. _____

6. _____

7. _____

8. _____

 The long **i** sound can be spelled **i_e** as in size, **ie** as in pies, **ia** as in dial, and **i__** as in pint.

List Words

tried
drive
size
pies
island
inside

Circle each **list word** that is misspelled. Write the misspelled words correctly on the lines.

1. Dad baked five apple pise. _____

2. We heard a noise coming from insid the box. _____

3. An iland is completely surrounded by water. _____

4. I treid to catch the cat, but she was too fast. _____

5. This shoe doesn't look like the right siz for my foot. _____

6. Mom will driev us to school. _____

Show What You Know

One word is misspelled in each set of **list words**. Fill in the circle next to the list word that is spelled incorrectly.

1. ○ drive   ○ giant   ○ bottom   ○ awaik
2. ○ since   ○ ice   ○ waggon   ○ island
3. ○ fases   ○ alive   ○ its   ○ baked
4. ○ life   ○ past   ○ kannot   ○ magic
5. ○ train   ○ pies   ○ grinde   ○ does
6. ○ level   ○ sister   ○ diet   ○ rok
7. ○ places   ○ nekst   ○ daily   ○ give
8. ○ tride   ○ cried   ○ kill   ○ under
9. ○ pirson   ○ blame   ○ quite   ○ claim
10. ○ jale   ○ pick   ○ main   ○ dial
11. ○ insied ○ fast   ○ them   ○ once
12. ○ safe   ○ wuter   ○ forest   ○ cage
13. ○ pint   ○ paint   ○ felt   ○ coller
14. ○ nine   ○ rase   ○ fire   ○ case
15. ○ died   ○ age   ○ klimb   ○ paid
16. ○ mail   ○ dead   ○ mark   ○ rize
17. ○ size   ○ gon   ○ danger   ○ egg
18. ○ beside ○ burd   ○ little   ○ tale
19. ○ explain ○ dug   ○ goble   ○ awake
20. ○ faces   ○ next   ○ dayly   ○ jail

Spelling Words in Action

What kind of store is in this building?

Musical Art

The wall is alive with the sight of **music**! Music is a **tune** that you hear, isn't it? Yes, but you can also see music. A musician writes notes on a page for other people to sing or play. Perhaps you **know** someone who can play a **flute** or a piano by reading musical notes.

The tune on the wall in the picture has to be one of the world's largest. Is it a **joke** by a singing sign painter? No. It's a mural. That's a special kind of painting that is done on a wall.

This **huge** mural is five stories high! Why would anyone put so much music on the side of a building? The store **owner** wanted people to know what he was selling. He **used** giant notes to let folks know. The building is a music store in Minneapolis, Minnesota! Perhaps if you're walking by the building, you may just feel like singing!

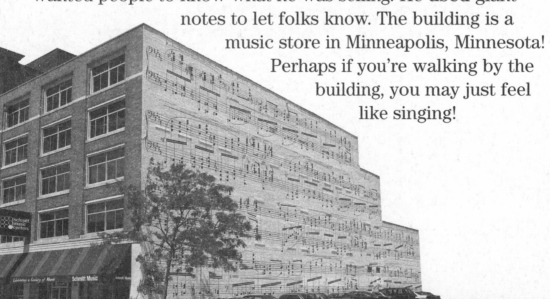

Say each word in dark print in the selection. Listen for the long o and the long u sounds. What do you notice about the way they are spelled?

TIP

The long **o** sound can be spelled
o_e as in <u>stone</u>,
oa as in <u>load</u>,
ow as in <u>know</u>, and
o_ _ as in <u>only</u>.
The long **u** sound can be spelled
u_e as in <u>tune</u>,
ue as in <u>true</u>, and
u as in <u>music</u>.

Spelling Practice

Long-Vowel Sounds <u>o</u> and <u>u</u>

Write each **list word** under the correct heading.

long **o** spelled **o_e**

1. _____ 2. _____

long **o** spelled **o_ _**

3. _____ 4. _____

long **o** spelled **ow**

5. _____ 6. _____

long **o** spelled **oa**

7. _____

long **u** spelled **ue**

8. _____

long **u** spelled **u**

9. _____ 10. _____

long **u** spelled **u_e**

11. _____

12. _____

13. _____

14. _____

15. _____

LIST WORDS

1. human   *human*
2. joke   *joke*
3. load   *load*
4. music   *music*
5. stone   *stone*
6. huge   *huge*
7. tune   *tune*
8. fumes   *fumes*
9. know   *know*
10. only   *only*
11. used   *used*
12. mostly   *mostly*
13. true   *true*
14. flute   *flute*
15. owner   *owner*

Missing Words

Write a **list word** to complete each sentence.

1. Our school band played beautiful _____.

2. The giant balloon looked _____ when it landed.

3. Do you _____ where I can find a pencil sharpener?

4. The little tree is _____ three-feet tall.

5. Everyone laughed when we played a _____ on the class.

6. The statue was so real it almost seemed _____.

Puzzle

Write the **list word** whose meaning matches each clue.

ACROSS

1. rock

3. a person

6. not false

8. something that is carried

9. mainly

DOWN

2. person who owns something

4. not new

5. musical instrument

6. melody

7. gas, smoke, or vapors

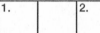

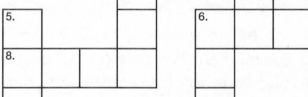

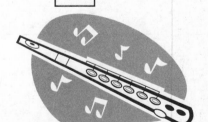

Spelling and Writing

Proofreading

Each sentence below has two mistakes. Use the proofreading marks to fix each mistake. Write the misspelled **list words** correctly on the lines.

1. Do you kno that the mural is huge

2. The painter uzed mostely big brushes.

3. The brushes were quite a lode for one

   hueman to carry alone.

4. The store oner plays the floote.

5. Many people thought the sign was onley

   a joak.

1. _____

2. _____

   _____

3. _____

   _____

4. _____

   _____

5. _____

   _____

Writing a Personal Narrative

How do you feel about music? Use the **list words** to write a short personal narrative telling what kind of music you like and why. Don't forget to proofread your paragraph. Fix any mistakes.

_____

_____

_____

_____

BONUS WORDS

coach

polite

cube

mute

total

Long-Vowel Sound e

Spelling Words in Action

What is Earth Savers?

Earth Savers

Have you ever noticed how **easily** your room gets messy if you don't clean things up right away? Your room is your own environment, but everything around us is part of the Earth's environment. The plants and animals, the water we drink, and the air we **breathe** are all a part of the Earth. With over six billion **people** sharing the world, the planet can get pretty dirty. That's why we all have to make a special effort to protect the Earth's environment.

Earth Savers is a club for kids that is helping to keep things clean. It was started by the National Wildlife Federation. With Earth Savers, kids help to protect nature and wildlife. There are club chapters in every state. Members form a **team** that cleans up places like a polluted stream or a beach. They **even** clean city **streets** and set up programs for recycling. To find out more about Earth Savers, **read** the information on their Web site (www.nwf.org/earthsavers).

Say each word in dark print in the selection. Listen for the long e sound. What do you notice about the ways the long e̅ is spelled?

TIP

The long e sound can be spelled
ea as in <u>read</u>,
ee as in <u>seen</u>,
eo as in <u>people</u>, and
e_e as in <u>even</u>.

Spelling Practice

LIST WORDS

1. read	*read*
2. seen	*seen*
3. team	*team*
4. east	*east*
5. seat	*seat*
6. steel	*steel*
7. streets	*streets*
8. people	*people*
9. breathe	*breathe*
10. beach	*beach*
11. easily	*easily*
12. even	*even*
13. elect	*elect*
14. greeting	*greeting*
15. meaning	*meaning*

Long-Vowel Sound <u>e</u>

Write each **list word** under the correct heading.

Long **e** spelled **ea**

1. _____
2. _____
3. _____
4. _____
5. _____
6. _____
7. _____
8. _____

Long **e** spelled **ee**

9. _____
10. _____
11. _____
12. _____

Long **e** spelled **eo**

13. _____

Long **e** spelled **e_e**

14. _____ 15. _____

Missing Words

Write a **list word** to complete each sentence.

1. There are six billion _____ living on the Earth.

2. We watched the waves crash upon the sandy _____.

3. The basketball _____ traveled to the next town to play.

4. The class will _____ a new president for next year.

5. The strongman lifted the _____ bar high above his head.

6. Please _____ the story carefully.

Puzzle

Write the **list word** whose meaning matches each clue.

ACROSS

4. flat or level

6. take in air

7. roads

8. to have used your eyes

DOWN

1. a place to sit

2. saying hello

3. what is understood

5. without trying too hard

9. not west

Spelling and Writing

Proofreading

Each sentence below has two mistakes. Use the proofreading marks to fix each mistake. Write the misspelled **list words** correctly on the lines.

1. Many peopel helped clean our city's streats.

2. even the children joined the teem.

3. With cleaner air we can all breeth more easaly.

4. it's important to ealect someone who cares about the environment.

1. _____

_____

2. _____

3. _____

4. _____

_____

Writing a Paragraph

Pretend that you are creating a Web page about the environment. Write a paragraph using as many **list words** as you can to persuade people to join your own save-the-Earth club. Be sure to proofread your work. Fix any mistakes.

_____

_____

_____

_____

_____

_____

_____

BONUS WORDS

seashore

reason

season

speedy

leaning

Spelling Words in Action

Is a smile or a frown easier for your face to make?

Put on a Happy Face

The more you crack it the more people like it. That's what a **smile** is all about. Did you know that **frowning** is harder than smiling? A frown uses 43 of the muscles in your face. It takes only 17 muscles to smile. Why would you want to **spend** your time frowning anyway? By smiling, you could **bring** some joy to yourself and others as well. So smile—it's easy. Put on a happy face, and make some new **friends**.

Smiling is good for your health, too. Doctors believe that laughing helps sick people feel better. They say that laughing actually makes their bodies get well, too! **Best** of all, a smile is **free**! So keep smiling.

Say each word in dark print in the selection. What consonant sounds do you hear at the beginning of the words? What consonant sounds do you hear at the end of best?

TIP

A **consonant blend** is two or more consonants that come together in a word. Their sounds blend together, but each sound is heard. A blend can come at the beginning or end of a word.

S blends	R blends	L blends
sm as in <u>sm</u>ile	fr as in <u>fr</u>ee	bl as in <u>bl</u>ind
sp as in <u>sp</u>end	cr as in <u>cr</u>eek	fl as in <u>fl</u>oat
st as in be<u>st</u>	br as in <u>br</u>ing	pl as in <u>pl</u>ant

Spelling Practice

Words with Consonant Blends

Write the **list words** that begin or end with **s** blends. One word has both an **s** blend and an **l** blend.

1. _____
2. _____
3. _____
4. _____
5. _____
6. _____

Write the **list words** that begin with **r** blends.

7. _____
8. _____
9. _____
10. _____
11. _____

Write the **list words** that begin with **l** blends.

12. _____
13. _____
14. _____
15. _____
16. _____

LIST WORDS

1. smile — *smile*
2. smart — *smart*
3. best — *best*
4. free — *free*
5. spend — *spend*
6. blind — *blind*
7. float — *float*
8. plant — *plant*
9. slumber — *slumber*
10. sting — *sting*
11. frowning — *frowning*
12. friends — *friends*
13. creek — *creek*
14. glue — *glue*
15. bring — *bring*

Missing Words

Write a **list word** to complete each sentence.

1. This is the _____ ice cream I have ever tasted.

2. Can you _____ on your back in the water?

3. The muddy _____ flowed into the big lake.

4. On Saturday night, we are having a _____ party.

5. Be _____. Study before you take the test.

6. The sad clown was _____ during the whole show.

7. Craig's _____ visited him in the hospital.

8. Please _____ your notebook when you come to class.

Scrambled Letters

Unscramble the letters to spell **list words**. Print one letter in each box. Then, read down the shaded boxes to answer the riddle.

1. dlnbi

2. egul

3. talnp

4. tisgn

5. dpens

6. erfe

7. miles

Riddle: What is at the beginning of everything,

At the end of every <u>mile</u>,

At the beginning of every <u>end</u>,

And at the end of every <u>smile</u>?   **Answer:** It is the _____.

Spelling and Writing

Proofreading

Each sentence below has two mistakes. Use the proofreading marks to fix each mistake. Write the misspelled **list words** correctly on the lines.

Proofreading Marks

⬭ spelling mistake

≡ capital letter

⊙ add period

1. my family will spende Saturday at the circus.

1. _____

2. I get to bering my freands with me.

2. _____

_____

3. children get in frea that day.

3. _____

4. No frouning allowed when you see the clowns

4. _____

5. Those trained elephants are really snart

5. _____

6. we all smyile when we see the lions.

6. _____

Writing a Description

What makes you laugh? How does laughing make you feel? Write a brief paragraph that describes your feelings. Use as many **list words** as you can. Be sure to proofread your paragraph. Fix any mistakes.

_____

_____

_____

_____

_____

BONUS WORDS

crack

stem

glide

blast

freeze

Spelling Words in Action

What is the National Cowboy Poetry Gathering?

Poetry Round Up

Every year, thousands of cowpokes **plan** a **trip** to a small Nevada town. These gals and guys come for a different **kind** of rodeo. It's a rodeo of rhyme! They call it the National Cowboy Poetry Gathering. This **special** event brings together folks who not only enjoy poetry, but also those who **blaze** the western trails. They write about things like animals, **fresh** air, and life on the open range! Here's a sample of their kind of poetic horseplay:

"To My Horse, Whinny"

There are other colts in my corral,
Among them you're the best.
You're faithful, loyal, my best pal,
And hooves beyond the rest!
Of all the ponies in the race,
I'm sure that you would beat 'em
I'd really like to bring you **flowers**,
But I know you'd only eat 'em.
And I will love you for all time,
I'm stating here and now.
I'm writing you this round-up rhyme,
'Cause you're prettier than a cow.

Look back at the words in dark print. Can you name the consonant blend in each word?

TIP

In a **consonant blend**, you can hear the sounds of two or more letters together in a word. Listen for the blends in these words:

sp as in <u>sp</u>ecial   **tr** as in <u>tr</u>ip
pl as in <u>pl</u>an   **nd** as in ki<u>nd</u>

Spelling Practice

LIST WORDS

1. trip — *trip*
2. drove — *drove*
3. plan — *plan*
4. kind — *kind*
5. floors — *floors*
6. melting — *melting*
7. blaze — *blaze*
8. spill — *spill*
9. flowers — *flowers*
10. Friday — *Friday*
11. frozen — *frozen*
12. please — *please*
13. broken — *broken*
14. fresh — *fresh*
15. special — *special*

Words with Consonant Blends

Write the **list words** that have **r** blends.

1. _____
2. _____
3. _____
4. _____
5. _____
6. _____

Write the **list words** that have **l** blends.

7. _____
8. _____
9. _____
10. _____
11. _____
12. _____

Write the **list words** that have **s** blends.

13. _____
14. _____

Write the **list word** that has an **n** blend.

15. _____

Word Meaning

Write the **list word** that matches each meaning.

1. to satisfy _____

2. split into pieces _____

3. sort or variety _____

4. a way to do something _____

5. changing form from solid to liquid _____

6. the bottom parts of rooms _____

7. to flow over _____

8. newly made _____

Missing Words

Write **list words** to finish the story. The letter shapes will help you.

☐☐☐☐☐ was a ☐☐☐☐☐☐ day.

Dad ☐☐☐☐☐ us to the lake. The lake was

☐☐☐☐☐. Inside the cabin, Mom and I lit a fire. In the

morning, the ice on the lake was ☐☐☐☐☐☐☐. We even

saw pretty, purple ☐☐☐☐☐☐ peeping through the snow.

Spelling and Writing

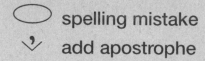

Proofreading

Each sentence below has two mistakes. Use the proofreading marks to fix each mistake. Write the misspelled **list words** correctly on the lines.

Proofreading Marks

◯ spelling mistake

∨ add apostrophe

1. We took a tripp west in Dads new car.

1._____

2. On Fridae, we droev through the mountains.

2._____

_____

3. It was so cold, my sisters face felt frosen.

3._____

4. Our plann was to stop at my aunts ranch.

4._____

5. When we got there, we had some of her special freash bread.

5._____

_____

Writing a Poem

Poems can be serious or funny. They can rhyme or not rhyme. Poems can be about anything you want them to be. Use the **list words** to write a poem of your own. Be sure to proofread your poem. Fix any mistakes.

BONUS WORDS

treasure

plane

depend

spare

frost

_____

_____

_____

_____

Spelling Words in Action

When is a dog not really a dog?

Prairie Pups

They look like squirrels, but they bark like little dogs. They have **pretty** grayish-brown coats, and they're very cute. What are they? They're prairie dogs!

It seems as if these **playful** little animals have **always** been around. They have been seen popping out of holes since the days when North America was being settled. Although we call them dogs, they are really ground squirrels. They live together underground in a large group called a town. Digging room after room, they make space for their **very** large **family**. One town can have more than a thousand prairie dogs.

Prairie dogs eat grass and roots. These hungry animals can cause **plenty** of trouble for farmers. **Maybe** you'll find this hard to believe, but they get most of the water they need from the plants. Have you ever heard of a prairie dog asking for a drink of water?

Look back at the words in dark print. What do you notice about their spellings? Say each word. What vowel sound does the y stand for in each word?

In some words, **y** teams up with the letter **a** to spell the long-vowel sound **a**, as in <u>maybe</u>. At the end of a word with more than one syllable, **y** may make the long-vowel sound **e** as in <u>pretty</u>. Listen for the sound that **y** makes in each **list word**.

Spelling Practice

LIST WORDS

1. lady   *lady*
2. playful   *playful*
3. always   *always*
4. very   *very*
5. empty   *empty*
6. angry   *angry*
7. any   *any*
8. anyway   *anyway*
9. maybe   *maybe*
10. carry   *carry*
11. family   *family*
12. pretty   *pretty*
13. plenty   *plenty*
14. heavy   *heavy*
15. hungry   *hungry*

Vowel Sounds of <u>y</u>

Write the **list words** in which **y** spells the long **e** sound. One word has both the long **e** and the long **a** sound.

1. _____
2. _____
3. _____
4. _____
5. _____
6. _____
7. _____
8. _____
9. _____
10. _____
11. _____
12. _____

Write the **list words** in which **ay** spells the long **a** sound.

13. _____   14. _____

15. _____   16. _____

Syllables

Each **list word** below has been divided into syllables. Say each word. Put an accent mark (´) after the syllable with the strong sound.
Then, write the **list words**.

In a dictionary, an accent mark appears after the syllable with the strong sound.

plen´ ty

1. ver y _____

2. car ry _____

3. may be _____

4. fam i ly _____

5. an gry _____

6. hun gry _____

7. an y way _____

8. emp ty _____

Word Puzzle

Write the **list word** whose meaning matches each clue.
Then, use the number code to answer the riddle.

1. hard to lift ___ ___ ___ ___ ___
           2

2. frisky; full of fun ___ ___ ___ ___ ___ ___ ___
                        3

3. at all times ___ ___ ___ ___ ___ ___
                   4

4. all that is needed ___ ___ ___ ___ ___ ___
            5

5. parents and children ___ ___ ___ ___ ___ ___
                  1

6. pleasant to look at ___ ___ ___ ___ ___ ___

7. wanting food ___ ___ ___ ___ ___ ___

8. having nothing in it ___ ___ ___ ___ ___
                   6

Riddle: What do you call a quiet little dog?

Answer: ___ ___ ___ ___ ___ ___ ___ ___ ___ ___
       1   2   3   4   2   5   3   5   5   6

Spelling and Writing

Proofreading

Proofreading Marks

⬯ spelling mistake

℮ take out something

Each sentence below has two mistakes. Use the proofreading marks to fix each mistake. Write the misspelled **list words** correctly on the lines.

1. Prairie dogs can be playfulle, but they work vary hard, too.

1. _____

_____

2. A prairie dog allwaes starts its home by digging a a tunnel.

2. _____

3. At the end of of the tunnel, mayby it will make a sleeping room.

3. _____

4. Prairie dog towns have plente of entrances so the the animals can easily escape from danger.

4. _____

Writing a Description

The prairie dog towns and colorful flowers make the prairie a very interesting place. Write a description of where you live, a playground, or your favorite park. Tell what you would see, hear, or smell in that place. Try to use as many **list words** as you can. Be sure to proofread your description. Fix any mistakes.

_____

_____

_____

_____

BONUS WORDS

holiday

sixty

country

easy

Monday

In lessons 7 through 11, you learned to spell words with the long-vowel sounds **o**, **u**, and **e**, and with **y** as a vowel. You also learned to spell words with consonant blends.

Check Your Spelling Notebook

Look at the words in your spelling notebook. Which words for lessons 7 through 11 did you have the most trouble with? Write them here.

_____

_____

Practice writing your troublesome words with a partner. Try writing invisible letters for each word with your finger on your partner's back. Your partner can say the letters aloud as you write.

Lesson 7

Long vowels often have the same sounds as their letter names. The long **o** sound can be spelled **o_e** as in <u>stone</u>, **oa** as in <u>load</u>, **ow** as in <u>know</u>, and **o_ _** as in <u>only</u>. The long **u** sound can be spelled **u_e** as in <u>tune</u>, **ue** as in <u>true</u>, and **u** as in <u>music</u>.

Write a **list word** that means the same or almost the same as each word given. One word will not be used.

List Words

mostly
joke
huge
stone
music
human
flute

1. person _____

2. musical instrument _____

3. rock _____

4. big _____

5. song _____

6. mainly _____

The long **e** sound can be spelled **ea** as in <u>read</u>, **ee** as in <u>seen</u>, **eo** as in <u>people</u>, and **e_e** as in <u>even</u>.

List Words

people

steel

read

seat

greeting

beach

east

Write a **list word** that rhymes with each word given. One word will not be used.

1. teach _____

2. meat _____

3. bead _____

4. beast _____

5. meeting _____

6. peel _____

 A **consonant blend** is two or more consonants that come together in a word. Their sounds blend together, but each sound is heard. You can hear the consonant blends in <u>smart</u>, <u>glue</u>, and <u>free</u>.

List Words

smile

best

spend

sting

float

friends

bring

Write a **list word** that means the opposite of each word or phrase given. One word will not be used.

1. sink _____

2. worst _____

3. take away _____

4. frown _____

5. enemies _____

6. save _____

You can hear the sounds of two or more letters together in a **consonant blend**. Listen for the blends in <u>trip</u>, <u>plan</u>, <u>spill</u>, and <u>kind</u>.

Write a **list word** that matches each clue. One word will not be used.

List Words

kind
floors
blaze
Friday
fresh
please
special

1. are walked on _____

2. not like all the rest _____

3. sweet and nice _____

4. nice word when you ask _____

5. the last school day of the week _____

6. what a fire is _____

 In some words, **y** helps to spell the long **a** sound as in <u>playful</u>. The letter **y** may also spell the long **e** sound at the end of a word with more than one syllable, as in <u>pretty</u>.

One word is misspelled in each set of **list words**. Circle the word that is wrong. Then, write it correctly on the line.

List Words

anyway
hungry
family
heavy
maybe
always

1. anyway   heavy   family _____

2. allways   maybe   anyway _____

3. hungry   haevy   family _____

4. always   maybe   aneyway _____

5. family   hungery   always _____

6. heavy   maybee   hungry _____

Show What You Know

One word is misspelled in each set of **list words**. Fill in the circle next to the **list word** that is spelled incorrectly.

1. ○ human   ○ kind   ○ loed   ○ lady
2. ○ smile   ○ streats   ○ seat   ○ mostly
3. ○ flouers   ○ any   ○ easily   ○ blaze
4. ○ spend   ○ used   ○ heevy   ○ broken
5. ○ friends   ○ greting   ○ read   ○ fumes
6. ○ flote   ○ east   ○ best   ○ very
7. ○ plenty   ○ melting   ○ Frida   ○ music
8. ○ empty   ○ slumber   ○ please   ○ gloo
9. ○ even   ○ always   ○ fresh   ○ kno
10. ○ floors   ○ stone   ○ plaiful   ○ frozen
11. ○ angry   ○ team   ○ breethe   ○ joke
12. ○ free   ○ speshul   ○ creek   ○ people
13. ○ only   ○ pretty   ○ beach   ○ frouning
14. ○ floot   ○ true   ○ hungry   ○ sting
15. ○ elect   ○ mebbe   ○ steel   ○ anyway
16. ○ hyooj   ○ meaning   ○ trip   ○ tune
17. ○ owner   ○ spill   ○ plane   ○ droav
18. ○ carry   ○ blind   ○ smarte   ○ plant
19. ○ bring   ○ load   ○ sene   ○ streets
20. ○ flowers   ○ greeting   ○ famly   ○ float

Spelling Words in Action

What kind of things have people used as money?

Funny Money

Money hasn't always been the coins and bills we have today. At one time or another, almost anything could have been used for money. In fact, money could have been anything people used to **buy** and sell things. In India, brightly colored shells were used as money. The Fijians used whales' teeth. In the ancient Roman **army**, soldiers were paid with lumps of salt.

The island of Manhattan in New York City was bought by the Dutch from Native Americans. According to legend, in a **sly** move, the Dutch paid with glass beads. The island turned out to be worth quite a bit more than beads! That was in 1626. Today, **every** time we buy something, we use paper money printed by the government.

Many board games use "play" money. Of course we can't forget **candy** coins made out of chocolate. If **anyone** tried to spend it, they would probably take a bite first!

Look back at the words in dark print. Say each word. What vowel sound does the y spell or help to spell in each word?

The letter **y** can spell or help spell the long-vowel sounds **i** and **e**. In one-syllable words, **y** spells long **i**, as in <u>shy</u>, <u>buy</u>, and <u>eye</u>. In words with more syllables, **y** often spells the long **e** sound, as in <u>army</u> and <u>anyone</u>.

Spelling Practice

LIST WORDS

1. army   *army*
2. anyone   *anyone*
3. twenty   *twenty*
4. shy   *shy*
5. candy   *candy*
6. dry   *dry*
7. body   *body*
8. money   *money*
9. buy   *buy*
10. honey   *honey*
11. every   *every*
12. eye   *eye*
13. sly   *sly*
14. turkey   *turkey*
15. chimney   *chimney*

y as a Vowel

Write the **list words** in which **y** spells or helps to spell the long **e** sound.

1. _____
2. _____
3. _____
4. _____
5. _____
6. _____
7. _____
8. _____
9. _____
10. _____

Write the **list words** in which **y** spells or helps to spell the long **i** sound.

11. _____
12. _____
13. _____
14. _____
15. _____

Scrambled Letters

Unscramble the letters to make **list words**.

1. hys _____
2. yee _____
3. ryd _____
4. yub _____
5. hiceynm _____
6. aenoyn _____
7. boyd _____

8. yeohn _____
9. revey _____
10. tnwyte _____

Definitions

Write the **list word** that matches each meaning.

1. a big bird _____
2. a sweet food _____
3. any person _____
4. a large group of soldiers _____
5. the main part of a person or animal _____
6. a pipe used to release smoke _____
7. crafty or sneaky _____
8. not wet _____
9. one more than nineteen _____
10. all _____

Spelling and Writing

Proofreading

Proofreading Marks

⬭ spelling mistake

⊙ add period

⌃ add something

Each sentence below has two mistakes. Use the proofreading marks to fix each mistake. Write the misspelled **list words** correctly on the lines.

1. At one time, people used shells as monee

2. Rare feathers and huney were used in trade

3. Who hadthe sliy idea to use paper?

4. Would my turkee feather beworth something?

1. _____

2. _____

3. _____

4. _____

Writing a Paragraph

If you could choose one thing to use instead of money, what would it be? Write a paragraph to convince others that your form of "money" is the best. Use as many **list words** as you can. Be sure to proofread your paragraph. Fix any mistakes.

_____

_____

_____

_____

BONUS WORDS

aye

spy

hockey

everybody

anyhow

Spelling Words in Action

What U.S. Championship did Stanley Newman win?

The Crossword Kid

In a very short time, Stanley Newman won $1,500 and a six-foot long pencil! He won these prizes thanks to a lot of practice and a **sharp** mind. Stanley won the first U.S. Open Crossword Puzzle Championship. He finished a puzzle in **thirteen** minutes and twenty seconds.

Stanley beat the other 260 players who were the best "puzzlers" in the country. No one wanted **fourth** or **fifth** place. Not even second or third place would do. Everyone wanted first prize. When it came to the last and hardest puzzle, only a few players were left.

In the end, Stanley Newman was the big winner. He had to **rush** to **finish** within the fifteen-minute time limit, but he was able to **dash** off the answers faster **than** anyone. He did make one small mistake, but that didn't lose him the match. It only proves that nobody's perfect!

Look back at the words in dark print. Say each word. Can you find two consonants together in each word that make only one sound?

Spelling Practice

LIST WORDS

1. short   *short*
2. thaw   *thaw*
3. sharp   *sharp*
4. thirty   *thirty*
5. fourth   *fourth*
6. fifth   *fifth*
7. rush   *rush*
8. dash   *dash*
9. than   *than*
10. that   *that*
11. thinking   *thinking*
12. push   *push*
13. shape   *shape*
14. thirteen   *thirteen*
15. finish   *finish*
16. thumb   *thumb*
17. sixth   *sixth*
18. shadow   *shadow*
19. shine   *shine*
20. shovel   *shovel*

Words with <u>sh</u> and <u>th</u>

Write the **list words** that begin with **sh**.

1. _____   2. _____

3. _____   4. _____

5. _____   6. _____

Write the **list words** that end with **sh**.

7. _____   8. _____

9. _____   10. _____

Write the **list words** that begin with **th**.

11. _____   12. _____

13. _____   14. _____

15. _____   16. _____

17. _____

Write the **list words** that end with **th**.

18. _____   19. _____

20. _____

Write the **list word** whose meaning matches each clue.

ACROSS

3. 4th
5. using the mind
6. the person or thing mentioned
8. form or figure
9. glow

DOWN

1. fifteen minus two
2. twenty plus ten
3. end
4. 5th
7. compared to

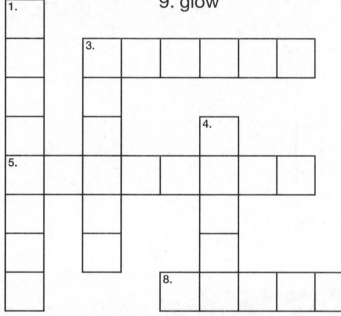

Dictionary

Write the **list words** that would appear on a dictionary page that has the following guide words. Write the entries in alphabetical order.

run/should

1. _____

2. _____

3. _____

4. _____

5. _____

6. _____

Spelling and Writing

Proofreading

The following article has eight mistakes. Use the proofreading marks to fix each mistake. Write the misspelled **list words** correctly on the lines.

Proofreading Marks

⬭ spelling mistake

≡ capital letter

⌃ add something

    arthur Wynne created the first crossword puzzle in 1913. His idea came from agame he remembered called Magic Square.
In a very shorte time, wynne's own puzzle began to take shaip. When it was completed, he knew thet it would take a sharpe mind to solve it. Wynne's puzzle was so popular that soon people everywhere were in a rushe to buy crossword-puzzle books.

1. _____

2. _____

3. _____

4. _____

5. _____

Writing a Description

Puzzles are a lot of fun, and there are many kinds to choose from. There are crossword puzzles, word-search puzzles, and jigsaw puzzles. Use the **list words** to describe your favorite puzzle. Tell why you like it. Be sure to proofread your writing. Fix any mistakes.

_____

_____

_____

_____

_____

_____

_____

BONUS WORDS

breathe

shoulder

shiver

thief

selfish

Spelling Words in Action

What is mahnomen?

Gift From the Creator

Although wild rice can be enjoyed **everywhere**, it holds special importance to the Ojibwa people of Minnesota. The Ojibwa **who** call the grain *mahnomen*, gather together **each** September for a very important harvest.

The harvest begins at daybreak when **whole** families go out to the rice beds. Harvesters travel in canoes. In every canoe, there are two people. **While** one person steers the canoe, the other uses a pair of wooden sticks. One stick is used to **catch** the stalk of grain and bend it over the canoe. The other stick is used to **whack** the stalks so that the rice falls into the canoe. The harvesters can tell **whether** the grain is ripe by how easily it falls from the stems.

Mahnomen, **which** means "the gift from the creator," is **rich** in vitamins. The food is not the only gift the Ojibwa receive from the harvest. As one harvester said, "The sweet thing about the wild rice harvest is that it brings families together."

Look back at the words in dark print. What sound does the consonant digraph <u>ch</u> make? What sounds does the consonant digraph <u>wh</u> make?

61

Spelling Practice

TIP

Consonant digraphs are pairs of consonants, such as **ch** or **wh**, that make one sound when they are written together. You can hear the **ch** sound in <u>each</u> and the **wh** sound in <u>whale</u>. In <u>who</u> and <u>whole</u>, the **w** is silent, but you hear the **h**.

LIST WORDS

1. wheel   *wheel*
2. whale   *whale*
3. everywhere   *everywhere*
4. which   *which*
5. each   *each*
6. check   *check*
7. while   *while*
8. chewy   *chewy*
9. rich   *rich*
10. chapter   *chapter*
11. chart   *chart*
12. catch   *catch*
13. whisper   *whisper*
14. who   *who*
15. whole   *whole*
16. bench   *bench*
17. whisk   *whisk*
18. whack   *whack*
19. whether   *whether*
20. pinch   *pinch*

Words with ch and wh

Write each **list word** under the correct sound of its consonant digraph. One word will be used twice.

ch as in <u>beach</u>

1. _____ 2. _____

3. _____ 4. _____

5. _____ 6. _____

7. _____ 8. _____

9. _____ 10. _____

wh as in <u>when</u>

11. _____ 12. _____

13. _____ 14. _____

15. _____ 16. _____

17. _____ 18. _____

19. _____

wh as in <u>whom</u>

20. _____ 21. _____

Word Meaning

Write the **list word** that matches each clue.

1. needing much chewing _____

2. a long, hard seat _____

3. to move or brush _____

4. part of a book _____

5. to take hold of _____

6. one piece; complete _____

7. very large sea animal _____

8. in all places _____

Scrambled Letters

Unscramble the letters to make **list words**. Then, use the number code to answer the riddle. Find the letter with the number 1 below it. Write that letter on the line above the number 1. Do the same for the other numbers.

1. chawk ___ ___ ___ ___
              9

2. ohw ___ ___ ___
              4

3. thewreh ___ ___ ___ ___ ___ ___ ___
                          2

4. priwseh ___ ___ ___ ___ ___ ___ ___
                                6

5. loweh ___ ___ ___ ___ ___
              8   3

6. elehw ___ ___ ___ ___ ___
              1   7

7. chinp ___ ___ ___ ___ ___
                          5

8. hawel ___ ___ ___ ___ ___
                      11 10

Riddle: What do you say when you meet a three-headed monster?

Answer: ___ ___ ___ ___ ___ ___ ___ ___ ___ ___ ___ ___ ___ ___
              1   2   3   3   4   5   6   7   7   8   9   10 11 11 8

Spelling and Writing

Proofreading

This paragraph has nine mistakes. Use the proofreading marks to fix each mistake. Write the misspelled **list words** correctly on the lines.

In a Hopi family's cornfield, wich they have farmed for many years, plants are evreeware. The Hopi dig small holes in the ground and put kernels in in eech hole they chek the plants daily to keep pests away. If there is enough rain, the harvest will be be ritch.

Proofreading Marks

⬭ spelling mistake

☰ capital letter

⊙ add period

℮ take out something

1. _____

2. _____

3. _____

4. _____

5. _____

Writing a Paragraph

Many foods are made of rice. There are rice cakes, rice pudding, and rice cereal. Think about the rice foods you like. Then, write a paragraph that describes your favorite. Use as many **list words** as you can.

_____

_____

_____

_____

_____

BONUS WORDS

whirl

whine

champion

witch

somewhat

Lesson 16

Spelling Words in Action

What are hieroglyphs?

The Art of Writing

Over 5,000 years ago, the ancient Egyptians started to write down their spoken language. The Egyptians **wrote** their language using pictures. These pictures are called hieroglyphs. Each hieroglyph stands for a different sound, idea, or object. Several hieroglyphs can stand for one letter.

Unlike English, hieroglyphs can be written in more than one direction. They can be written from left to right, like English, or right to left, like Arabic and Hebrew. They can also be written from top to bottom, like Chinese. You might ask how the ancient Egyptians kept **track** of which direction to read. What if they got the **wrong** meaning from a letter? The Egyptians **knew** by the pictures themselves. If the **sign** for a letter faced left, they started reading from the left. If the sign faced right, they started reading from the right.

A **writer** using Egyptian hieroglyphs would probably have a **rough** time telling a story. He or she would not only have to know how to write, but also how to draw!

Look back at the words in dark print. Say each word. Can you find two consonants together in each word that make only one sound?

TIP

The **n** sound can be spelled with **kn** or **gn**, as in <u>knew</u> and <u>sign</u>. The **r** sound can be spelled with **wr**, as in <u>wrote</u>. The **f** sound can be spelled with **gh** or **ph**, as in <u>rough</u> and <u>phone</u>. The **k** sound can be spelled with **ch** or **ck**, as in <u>school</u> and <u>wreck</u>.

LIST WORDS

1. school   *school*
2. wrote   *wrote*
3. phone   *phone*
4. knew   *knew*
5. sign   *sign*
6. knots   *knots*
7. wrong   *wrong*
8. knee   *knee*
9. knife   *knife*
10. wreck   *wreck*
11. wrap   *wrap*
12. knock   *knock*
13. rough   *rough*
14. laugh   *laugh*
15. elephant   *elephant*
16. cough   *cough*
17. wren   *wren*
18. writer   *writer*
19. graph   *graph*
20. track   *track*

Consonant Digraphs

Write the **list words** that spell each sound with a digraph. Then, circle the digraph in each word. Some words will be used more than once.

n as in <u>know</u> and <u>gnat</u>

1. _____
2. _____
3. _____
4. _____
5. _____
6. _____

f as in <u>photo</u> and <u>tough</u>

13. _____
14. _____
15. _____
16. _____
17. _____
18. _____

r as in <u>wrist</u>

7. _____
8. _____
9. _____
10. _____
11. _____
12. _____

k as in <u>luck</u> and <u>schooner</u>

19. _____
20. _____
21. _____
22. _____

Puzzle

Write the **list word** whose meaning matches each clue.

ACROSS
2. the bend in your leg
3. not correct
4. a person who writes
5. felt sure about
8. a place to learn
9. a chart

DOWN
1. used a pen and paper
2. rap on a door
3. a small bird
4. something that is broken
6. to put a cover around
7. take medicine for this

Missing Words

Write a **list word** from the box to finish each phrase.

| knots | knife | elephant | rough | laugh |

1. as sharp as a _____
2. as _____ as sandpaper
3. as big as an _____
4. the last _____
5. all tied up in _____

Spelling and Writing

Proofreading

This diary entry has eleven mistakes. Use the proofreading marks to fix each mistake. Write the misspelled **list words** correctly on the lines.

Dear Diary,

    Last week, my teacher called me on the fone and asked me to to write an article for the sckool paper. I was so excited! First, I made an outline to keep trak of my ideas Next, I wroat a ruff draft. Then, I proofread it it and fixed my mistakes. Finally, it was time to sine my name and turn it in. My teacher loved it! Well, Diary, today it appeared in the paper. Now I know what I want to be when I grow up—a riter

Proofreading Marks

◯ spelling mistake
⊙ add period
℮ take out something

1. _____

2. _____

3. _____

4. _____

5. _____

6. _____

7. _____

Writing a Message

Have you ever wanted to create your own secret language? If so, here's your chance. First, use the **list words** to write a secret message. Then, draw pictures or symbols to stand for each word. Be sure to proofread your secret message. Fix any mistakes.

_____

_____

_____

_____

_____

BONUS WORDS

knit

wrinkle

tough

cricket

anchor

Spelling Words in Action

Where was the first swamp-buggy race held?

Mud Machines

Splash! It's another buggy in the mud. What do you think is going on? You could call it a mud rodeo. Some people say it's the dirtiest race on Earth. It happens three times a year during Swamp Buggy Days in Naples, Florida. In late winter, **spring**, and again in the fall, the swamp buggies tune up for action.

Over fifty years ago, a man named Ed Frank started the swamp-buggy races. The first one was held in a muddy sweet-potato **patch**. Through the years, the buggies got better and faster. The news of the races **spread**, and people began to come from miles around. They wanted to see the crazy-looking machines with big tires and **strong** engines.

Today, the buggies race through "Mile-O-Mud" track. It runs through the swamp like a big figure eight. The drivers have to make sharp turns. There are lots of spills and **thrills**. Mud can **spray** in all directions while the fans **scream** with delight. It's all good, but not clean, fun!

Look back at the words in dark print. Say each word. Can you find the three consonants together in each word?

TIP

Three consonants together in a word make a **consonant cluster**. In many **list words**, **s** forms a cluster with two other letters. In some **list words**, **ch** or **th** forms a cluster with another letter.

Spelling Practice

LIST WORDS

1.	splash	*splash*
2.	spring	*spring*
3.	patch	*patch*
4.	strong	*strong*
5.	thrills	*thrills*
6.	spray	*spray*
7.	scream	*scream*
8.	throw	*throw*
9.	string	*string*
10.	struck	*struck*
11.	screen	*screen*
12.	itch	*itch*
13.	pitch	*pitch*
14.	spread	*spread*
15.	strawberry	*strawberry*
16.	stream	*stream*
17.	split	*split*
18.	scratch	*scratch*
19.	ditch	*ditch*
20.	thread	*thread*

Consonant Clusters

Complete each **list word** by writing a consonant cluster at the beginning or end of the word.

1. _____**ash** 2. _____**ead**

3. _____**ing** 4. _____**ong**

5. _____**it** 6. _____**awberry**

7. _____**ead** 8. _____**ills**

9. _____**ing** 10. _____**ow**

11. **pi**_____ 12. **pa**_____

13. _____**atch** 14. _____**uck**

15. **di**_____ 16. **i**_____

17. _____**eam** 18. _____**ay**

19. _____**een** 20. _____**eam**

Classification

Write the **list word** that belongs in each group.

1. fix, mend, _____
2. skin, rash, _____
3. fall, winter, _____
4. share, divide, _____
5. throw, toss, _____
6. joy, excitement, _____
7. string, ribbon, _____
8. brook, river, _____

Puzzle

Write a **list word** that matches each clue. Then, read down the shaded boxes to answer the riddle.

1. This word names a fruit. __ __ __ __ __ __ __

2. This will keep flies out of your home. __ __ __ __ __ __

3. This is a loud yell. __ __ __ __ __ __

4. This means "hit" __ __ __ __ __

5. This word names a deep hole. __ __ __ __ __ __

Riddle: What did the strawberry patch say to the rain?

Answer: If you keep this up, my name will

__ __ __ __ __ !

Spelling and Writing

Proofreading

The poster below has ten mistakes. Use the proofreading marks to fix each mistake. Write the misspelled **list words** correctly on the lines.

1. Where can you go to find thrilz and chills

2. Where else but Strawbarry Pache Beach for the annual Spreeng Fling.

3. Watch the amazing dune-buggy racers splasch through each wet, sandy dicth.

4. Skream for the winners when they reach the Finish line.

5. It all happens on June 23, beginning at 10 A.m.

1. _____

2. _____

_____

_____

3. _____

_____

4. _____

Writing a News Story

Imagine that you just attended the races at Swamp Buggy Days. Write a brief news report about what you saw. Include lots of colorful details. Use as many **list words** as you can. Be sure to proofread your news story. Fix any mistakes.

_____

_____

_____

_____

_____

BONUS WORDS

sprang

scramble

stranger

throne

hatch

In Lessons 13 through 17, you learned how to spell more words with **y** as a vowel. You also learned to spell words with consonant digraphs, such as **sh** and **ck**, and consonant clusters such as **str**.

Check Your Spelling Notebook

Look at the words in your spelling notebook. Which words for Lessons 13 through 17 did you have the most trouble with? Write them here.

_____

_____

Practice writing your troublesome words with a partner. Take turns spelling the words aloud while your partner writes the words on the board.

Lesson 13

 The letter **y** can spell the long **i** sound at the end of one-syllable words such as <u>shy</u>. At the end of two-syllable words, **y** can spell the long **e** sound as in <u>pretty</u>.

List Words

anyone

candy

twenty

army

money

buy

turkey

Write a **list word** that rhymes with each given word. One word will not be used.

1. twenty-one _____

2. plenty _____

3. jerky _____

4. sandy _____

5. my _____

6. honey _____

73

Two consonants can join together to form a consonant digraph, such as **th** in <u>thaw</u> and <u>then</u> and **sh** as in <u>short</u>.

List Words

push
shape
thaw
sharp
finish
short
rush

Write a **list word** that means the opposite of the word or phrase given. One word will not be used.

1. tall _____

2. freeze _____

3. pull _____

4. start _____

5. take your time _____

6. dull _____

 Listen for the consonant digraphs **ch** and **wh** in words such as <u>chewy</u>, <u>who</u>, and <u>whale</u>.

List Words

which
check
chart
whisper
whale
catch

Write the **list words** in alphabetical order.

1. _____

2. _____

3. _____

4. _____

5. _____

6. _____

Listen for the consonant digraphs in these words: <u>cough</u>, <u>knot</u>, <u>wrote</u>, and <u>phone</u>. A consonant digraph can come at the beginning, middle, or end of a word.

List Words

school

track

wrap

wrong

graph

rough

laugh

Write the **list word** that means the same or almost the same as each word given. One word will not be used.

1. incorrect _____

2. giggle _____

3. a place to learn _____

4. footprint _____

5. cover _____

6. bumpy _____

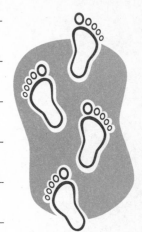

 Three consonants can join together to form a cluster. Listen for the consonant clusters in <u>split</u>, <u>itch</u>, and <u>thrills</u>.

List Words

spring

scream

stream

ditch

strong

throw

thread

Read the first two underlined words in each sentence. Write the **list word** that goes with the third underlined word in the same way. One word will not be used.

1. <u>big</u> is to <u>large</u> as <u>yell</u> is to _____

2. <u>cut</u> is to <u>scissors</u> as <u>sew</u> is to _____

3. <u>up</u> is to <u>down</u> as <u>catch</u> is to _____

4. <u>on</u> is to <u>off</u> as <u>weak</u> is to _____

5. <u>winter</u> is to <u>summer</u> as <u>fall</u> is to _____

6. <u>road</u> is to <u>street</u> as <u>creek</u> is to _____

Show What You Know

One word is misspelled in each set of **list words**. Fill in the circle next to the **list word** that is spelled incorrectly.

1. ○ thaw   ○ sign   ○ itch   ○ munny   ○ knock
2. ○ strong   ○ whisper   ○ dash   ○ shy   ○ bhench
3. ○ chapter   ○ sly   ○ writer   ○ thingking   ○ thread
4. ○ shape   ○ each   ○ elefant   ○ dry   ○ rough
5. ○ straberry   ○ struck   ○ wheel   ○ spread   ○ honey
6. ○ thumb   ○ chart   ○ phone   ○ patch   ○ chimmey
7. ○ stream   ○ evrywhere   ○ candy   ○ check   ○ whole
8. ○ shovel   ○ knee   ○ wheather   ○ ditch   ○ sharp
9. ○ foorth   ○ army   ○ fifth   ○ whack   ○ spray
10. ○ wren   ○ throw   ○ than   ○ rong   ○ buy
11. ○ knife   ○ skratch   ○ screen   ○ eye   ○ thirty
12. ○ graph   ○ catch   ○ rush   ○ string   ○ screem
13. ○ whale   ○ short   ○ laugh   ○ split   ○ shaddow
14. ○ who   ○ spulash   ○ body   ○ push   ○ knots
15. ○ turkey   ○ skool   ○ cough   ○ which   ○ pitch
16. ○ that   ○ wrote   ○ evury   ○ spring   ○ sixth
17. ○ chooie   ○ finish   ○ twenty   ○ while   ○ thrills
18. ○ knew   ○ ritch   ○ wreck   ○ pinch   ○ track
19. ○ whisk   ○ wrap   ○ shine   ○ thurteen   ○ money
20. ○ anywon   ○ bench   ○ elephant   ○ thinking   ○ strawberry

Spelling Words in Action

What has 1,000 heads?

A Green Giant

What is red and green and has 1,000 heads? Give up? It's one of the world's biggest salads. At least the people of Milford, Massachusetts, say it was the biggest. They tossed their giant salad for Milford's bicentennial. That was the **year** that Milford had its 200th birthday. The people in Milford **care** a lot about their town. They wanted to make something really **large**.

The people had to **start** planning months **before** the big day. First, they had to **order** all the things to make the salad. Then, from **morning** to evening, they chopped and sliced. A **cheer** went up from the crowd when they were finished. The salad had 1,000 heads of lettuce and a ton of tomatoes, cucumbers, olives, cheese, peppers, and onions.

On the day of the **party**, each guest lined up with a **fork** and plate. No one in Milford is sure if it was really the world's biggest salad, but for them, it was quite a mouthful!

Look back at the words in dark print in the selection. Say each word. What do you notice about the way the vowels sound in each word?

Spelling Practice

LIST-WORDS

1. year — *year*
2. care — *care*
3. large — *large*
4. start — *start*
5. before — *before*
6. order — *order*
7. party — *party*
8. fork — *fork*
9. cheer — *cheer*
10. chair — *chair*
11. garden — *garden*
12. morning — *morning*
13. compare — *compare*
14. clear — *clear*
15. appear — *appear*
16. court — *court*
17. course — *course*
18. pour — *pour*
19. prepare — *prepare*
20. fearless — *fearless*

Vowels with <u>r</u>

Write each **list word** under the correct heading.

ar sound as in <u>far</u>

1. _____
2. _____
3. _____
4. _____

er sound as in <u>air</u>

12. _____
13. _____
14. _____
15. _____

or sound as in <u>for</u>

5. _____
6. _____
7. _____
8. _____
9. _____
10. _____
11. _____

ir sound as in <u>ear</u>

16. _____
17. _____
18. _____
19. _____
20. _____

Classification

Write the **list word** that belongs in each group.

1. day, month, _____

2. big, huge, _____

3. celebration, gathering, _____

4. yell, shout, _____

5. desk, table, _____

6. fix up, get ready, _____

7. stadium, arena, _____

8. brave, courageous, _____

9. race, route, _____

Puzzle

Write the **list word** whose meaning matches each clue.

ACROSS

2. the early part of the day
5. to come into sight
6. earlier than
8. shout for joy
9. to begin
10. the way things are done

DOWN

1. to describe as being the same
3. a place for growing plants
4. without clouds
7. a tool for eating
8. to watch over

Spelling and Writing

Proofreading

Each sentence below has two mistakes. Use the proofreading marks to fix each mistake. Write the misspelled **list words** correctly on the lines.

Proofreading Marks

⬭ spelling mistake

≡ capital letter

1. my mother planted a vegetable gardin last year.

2. she asked me to help take kare of it.

3. I watered it befour school every mornin.

4. i made sure to keep the weeds cler.

5. The vegetables grew very larje that yer.

1. _____

2. _____

3. _____

_____

4. _____

5. _____

_____

Writing a Recipe

Imagine that you have been chosen to make a salad for the 200th birthday of your own town. What are you going to put in it? Write a recipe telling how to make your salad. Use as many **list words** as you can. Be sure to proofread your recipe. Fix any mistakes.

_____

_____

_____

_____

BONUS WORDS

darkness

airport

harm

forward

report

Spelling Words in Action

Why do people go to the National Hollerin' Contest?

Give a Hoot

Every year on the **third Saturday** in June, folks gather in Spivey's Corner, North Carolina, to hoot and holler. The people go there to **honor** the past by yelling!

Years ago around that part of the state, you could hear hollering every day. **Early** in the morning on their way to **work**, farmers would holler to each other. **First**, one farmer would yell. Then, another would take a turn. Several more would join in. Before long, people were hollering, from miles away. Each farmer would try to yell **better** and louder than the last. Each one had a special style. Neighbors would **learn** to recognize one another's yells. It was a signal that the workday was beginning.

Today, there's hardly any need to yell in Spivey's Corner. Now they have telephone **service**! Once a year though, people still holler. The best yellers come from all around. You could call Spivey's Corner the "hollerin' capital of the **world**."

Say the words in dark print in the selection. What vowel sound with r do you hear in each word?

TIP

The **ur** sound can be spelled many ways.

ir as in <u>first</u>   **ar** as in <u>sugar</u>

ear as in <u>learn</u>   **er** as in <u>paper</u>

or as in <u>worry</u>   **ur** as in <u>hurt</u>

Spelling Practice

LIST WORDS

1.	early	*early*
2.	third	*third*
3.	workbook	*workbook*
4.	first	*first*
5.	worry	*worry*
6.	hurt	*hurt*
7.	Saturday	*Saturday*
8.	better	*better*
9.	farmer	*farmer*
10.	honor	*honor*
11.	sugar	*sugar*
12.	nurse	*nurse*
13.	earth	*earth*
14.	paper	*paper*
15.	learn	*learn*
16.	world	*world*
17.	purse	*purse*
18.	curly	*curly*
19.	worse	*worse*
20.	service	*service*

Vowels with <u>r</u>

Write each **list word** under the correct spelling of the **ur** sound.

ir as in <u>birth</u>

1. _____

2. _____

ur as in <u>purr</u>

3. _____

4. _____

5. _____

6. _____

7. _____

ear as in <u>earn</u>

8. _____

9. _____

10. _____

er as in <u>later</u>

11. _____

12. _____

13. _____

14. _____

or as in <u>worm</u>

15. _____

16. _____

17. _____

18. _____

19. _____

ar as in <u>hangar</u>

20. _____

Dictionary Skills

Write the **list words** that would appear on a dictionary page that would have the guide words shown. Make sure the words are in alphabetical order.

better/hurt

1. _____

2. _____

3. _____

4. _____

5. _____

paper/worse

6. _____

7. _____

8. _____

9. _____

10. _____

Puzzle

Write the **list word** whose meaning matches each clue.

ACROSS
3. planter of crops
4. our planet
5. more excellent
7. gain knowledge
8. to be troubled
9. after second

DOWN
1. book of practice lessons
2. wound
4. not late
6. medical worker

Spelling and Writing

Proofreading

Each sentence below has two mistakes.
Use the proofreading marks to fix each mistake.
Write the misspelled **list words** correctly
on the lines.

Proofreading Marks
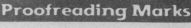

⬭ spelling mistake

⊙ add period

1. Many years ago, people in Africa used drums instead of papir to communicate

1. _____

2. They could lurn about other people bettur and faster with drums.

2. _____

_____

3. The drums could tell if someone was hert and if a doctor was needed

3. _____

4. The drums held a special place of honar among the people

4. _____

Writing a Poster

Use the **list words** to create a poster to advertise a contest you know about or would like to have. Remember to include important information such as what kind of contest it is, and where it will take place. Be sure to proofread your poster. Fix any mistakes.

_____

_____

_____

_____

BONUS WORDS

churn

earn

dessert

squirm

purple

Spelling Words in Action

What are these hunters hunting?

Hide and Seek

It's early fall in the forests of Oregon and Washington. For several weeks every year, armies of cone **hunters** search the woods. They look for pine **cones** with plenty of seeds. Lumber and seed companies pay them for the best cones. The seeds are used to plant new forests around the world.

The best cones grow on **branches** high in the trees. Hunters don't need to climb up to get the cones. They look for the places where squirrels hide cones. This way, they can get **bunches** of cones at a time. The hunter must think like a squirrel. Where would a squirrel hide food? Under a rock? Maybe under the **bushes**? Sometimes the hunters have to make several **passes** through the woods to fill their **boxes**.

Are the hunters stealing food from squirrels? "The squirrels will never go hungry," says one cone hunter. "They are too clever. We never find all of their hiding places. We might be just a few **inches** away from a hiding place and not find it. Besides, in addition to cones, squirrels also eat **berries** and nuts.

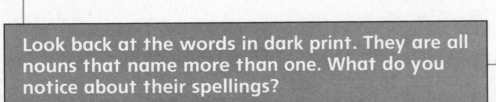

Look back at the words in dark print. They are all nouns that name more than one. What do you notice about their spellings?

TIP

Plural nouns name more than one person, place, or thing. If a noun ends in **x**, **s**, **sh**, or **ch**, add **es** to make it plural.

tax + **es** = taxes

class + **es** = classes

bush + **es** = bushes

branch + **es** = branches

If a noun ends with a consonant and **y**, change the **y** to **i** and add **es**.

baby + **es** = babies

LIST WORDS

1. cones   *cones*
2. hunters   *hunters*
3. desks   *desks*
4. babies   *babies*
5. berries   *berries*
6. puppies   *puppies*
7. bushes   *bushes*
8. bunches   *bunches*
9. brushes   *brushes*
10. branches *branches*
11. inches   *inches*
12. taxes   *taxes*
13. classes   *classes*
14. dishes   *dishes*
15. watches   *watches*
16. boxes   *boxes*
17. passes   *passes*
18. glasses   *glasses*
19. peaches   *peaches*
20. hobbies   *hobbies*

Making Plurals

Write each **list word** under the correct heading. The heading tells what to do to a singular word to form the plural **list word**.

add **es**	add **s**
1. _____	14. _____
2. _____	15. _____
3. _____	16. _____
4. _____	

change y to i, and add es

add **es**	change y to i, and add es
5. _____	17. _____
6. _____	18. _____
7. _____	19. _____
8. _____	20. _____
9. _____	
10. _____	
11. _____	
12. _____	
13. _____	

Word Meaning

Write the **list word** whose meaning matches each clue.

1. shells for holding ice cream _____
2. tools used for cleaning _____
3. baby dogs _____
4. subjects taken at school _____
5. units for measuring length _____
6. plates to eat from _____
7. fruit with large pits _____
8. containers for storing items _____
9. activities done in one's spare time _____
10. free tickets to an event _____
11. cups for holding liquids _____

Scrambled Letters

Unscramble the letters to spell **list words**. Print one letter in each box. Then, read down the shaded boxes to answer the riddle.

1. EREBRIS
2. SEATX

3. SERNBACH
4. SIABBE
5. CINSHE
6. AHETWCS

7. SKEDS
8. SIUPPEP
9. UNTRESH

Riddle: Why does a tree stand in the forest?

Answer: ___ ___ ___ ___ , ___ ___ ___ ___ ___ ___

Spelling and Writing

Proofreading

This article about squirrels has eight mistakes. Use the proofreading marks to fix the mistakes. Write the misspelled **list words** correctly on the lines.

   Baby squirrels hide in tree branchs until they feel brave enough to to climb down. The mother wachis over them as they explore. She shows them in which bushs tasty buntchas of beries can be found and how to gather coans for the winter. If danger is is near, the mother squirrel bravely drives off the enemy to protect her babies.

1. _____

2. _____

3. _____

4. _____

5. _____

6. _____

Writing a Description

Have you ever watched a squirrel or another wild animal? Write a description about what you saw. Use as many **list words** as you can. Be sure to proofread your description. Fix any mistakes.

_____

_____

_____

_____

_____

_____

Bonus Words

sweaters

butterflies

polishes

businesses

mixes

Spelling Words in Action

What did Rant Mullens use to make Bigfoot's "footprints"?

Trick Feet

In the state of Washington, folks tell about a giant monster. It's called Bigfoot of Mount Saint Helens. Over the years, its giant footprints have been seen by **men**, **women**, and **children**. Stories about the scary monster have shaken up the **lives** of many folks.

According to the story, Rant Mullens claimed to know the truth about Bigfoot. He said he started it himself as a joke in 1924. Using some **knives** and other tools, he carved two huge feet out of wood. Then, he used the wooden feet to make big footprints. He added mud and **leaves** to make the prints seem more believable.

It seems that his joke may have fooled people for almost sixty years! Rant might even be considered one of the local **heroes**. The joke, however, may be on Mr. Mullens. By creating fake tracks, he encouraged research into the possibility of a real Bigfoot. A scientist named Dr. Krantz studied many Bigfoot stories and tracks. Mr. Mullens' story may have helped to prove that perhaps a Bigfoot really does exist.

Look back at the words in dark print. All of these words are plural nouns. What is the singular form of each word?

89

TIP

Singular nouns ending with **f** or **fe** often form plurals by changing the **f** or **fe** to **v** and adding **es**.

life + es = lives.

Some plural nouns do not end in **s**. The spelling changes or stays the same.

goose→geese   man→men
mouse→mice   sheep→sheep

Spelling Practice

LIST WORDS

1. men   *men*
2. women   *women*
3. children   *children*
4. loaves   *loaves*
5. teeth   *teeth*
6. mice   *mice*
7. deer   *deer*
8. sheep   *sheep*
9. lives   *lives*
10. fish   *fish*
11. leaves   *leaves*
12. knives   *knives*
13. wolves   *wolves*
14. oxen   *oxen*
15. wives   *wives*
16. heroes   *heroes*
17. potatoes *potatoes*
18. geese   *geese*
19. shelves   *shelves*
20. cattle   *cattle*

Irregular Plurals

Write the **list words** that do not end with **s**.

1. _____   2. _____

3. _____   4. _____

5. _____   6. _____

7. _____   8. _____

9. _____   10. _____

11. _____

Write the **list words** that have singular forms that end with **f** or **fe**.

12. _____   13. _____

14. _____   15. _____

16. _____   17. _____

18. _____

Write the **list words** that have singular forms that end with the letter **o**.

19. _____   20. _____

Word Building

Build **list words** by replacing letters. Write the **list words**.

1. deal – al + er _____

2. twice – tw + m _____

3. worn – rn + men _____

4. with – wi + tee _____

5. shell – l + ves _____

6. lives – l + w _____

7. tomatoes – tom + pot _____

8. little – li + ca _____

9. loan – n + ves _____

10. lift – ft + ves _____

Word Puzzle

Write the **list word** whose meaning matches each clue. Then, read down the shaded boxes to answer the riddle.

Here's what they can do...

1. swim
2. say "baa"
3. fall off trees
4. live in woods

5. grow up
6. cut
7. be dads

8. fly
9. do brave deeds
10. howl at the moon
11. pull heavy carts

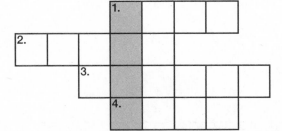
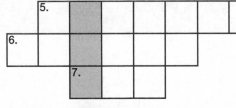
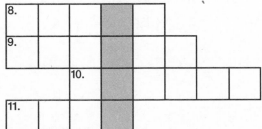

Riddle: What should you do if you meet a hungry monster?

Answer: ___ ___ ___ ___ ___ ___ ___ ___ ___ ___ ___ ___

Spelling and Writing

Proofreading

This informational story has eight mistakes. Use the proofreading marks to fix the mistakes. Write the misspelled **list words** correctly on the lines.

   In some parts of Asia, man, women, and childrun talk about the yeti, or the abominable snowman. The yeti supposedly lives in the high mountains. Those who claim to have seen it say that it is big and covered with hair like an Ape. What a sight It would be to see one! Some people think The yeti may just be large woolvs or some other animals that eat catel. What do you think

1. _____   2. _____

3. _____   4. _____

Writing a News Story

BONUS WORDS

Finding a real Bigfoot would be an amazing story. Write a make-believe newspaper story telling about your discovery of Bigfoot. Use as many **list words** as you can. Be sure to proofread your newspaper story. Fix any mistakes.

_____

_____

_____

_____

_____

bison

halves

scarves

buffaloes

thieves

Spelling Words in Action

Other than fire detection, what can a lookout tower be used for?

Above the Crowds

If you're in the mood for a mountain vacation, and you don't care to go **camping** in the woods, why not try a week in a lookout tower? In many national forests across the country, people are doing just that—vacationing in old fire towers.

At one time, the Forest Service **relied** heavily on these towers. From them, rangers **studied** the forest for signs of forest fire. Today, the Forest Service depends mostly on airplanes to look for fires. **Flying** over the trees, airplanes can pinpoint the exact locations of fires. As a result, many of the older lookout towers are no longer being used. Volunteers have begun **trying** to save these old towers. They have started **cleaning** and **repairing** them.

If you are **worried** about heights, a lookout tower is not the place for you. Many are five-stories high. There is no electricity, and you have to haul up your own water. There is also a little **swaying** in the breeze.

Look back at the words in dark print. What do you notice about their spellings? Did the base words change when an ending was added?

93

TIP

An ending is added at the end of a base word. If a word ends in a vowel and **y**, add only the ending—<u>pray</u> + **ed** = <u>prayed</u>. If a word ends in a consonant and **y**, change the **y** to **i** before adding the ending, unless the ending begins with **i**.

<u>worry</u> + **ed** = <u>worried</u>

<u>sway</u> + **ing** = <u>swaying</u>

Spelling Practice

LIST WORDS

1. rained   *rained*
2. prayed   *prayed*
3. studied   *studied*
4. cleaning   *cleaning*
5. thanked   *thanked*
6. acted   *acted*
7. worried   *worried*
8. helped   *helped*
9. copying   *copying*
10. flying   *flying*
11. hurried   *hurried*
12. married   *married*
13. dressing   *dressing*
14. camping   *camping*
15. replied   *replied*
16. trying   *trying*
17. repairing   *repairing*
18. swaying   *swaying*
19. spied   *spied*
20. multiplied   *multiplied*

Adding Endings to Base Words

Write the **list words**. In some **list words**, you must change the **y** to **i**.

1. rain + ed = _____
2. pray + ed = _____
3. study + ed = _____
4. clean + ing = _____
5. thank + ed = _____
6. act + ed = _____
7. worry + ed = _____
8. help + ed = _____
9. copy + ing = _____
10. fly + ing = _____
11. hurry + ed = _____
12. marry + ed = _____
13. dress + ing = _____
14. camp + ing = _____
15. reply + ed = _____
16. try + ing = _____
17. sway + ing = _____
18. repair + ing = _____
19. multiply + ed = _____
20. spy + ed = _____

Word Meaning

Read each sentence. Replace the underlined word or words with a **list word** that has the same meaning. Write the **list word** on the line.

1. We <u>rushed</u> to catch the bus. _____

2. We <u>learned about</u> volcanoes in science class. _____

3. I like <u>eating and sleeping in the woods</u>. _____

4. The sky turned gray and it <u>poured</u>. _____

5. My brother <u>performed</u> in his class play. _____

6. "Thank you," she <u>answered</u> when I gave her the book. _____

7. The mechanic spent two hours <u>fixing</u> the car. _____

8. The floor needed a good <u>scrubbing</u>. _____

Missing Words

Add **ing** or **ed** to a base word from the box to make **list words**. Write a **list word** to complete each sentence.

help	fly	copy	thank	sway
try	multiply	spy	worry	pray

1. I _____ my grandparents for the gift.

2. David _____ his dad do the housework.

3. I am _____ the words onto my paper now.

4. The farmers _____ for rain.

5. My parents were _____ when I came home late from school.

6. Todd is _____ to save his money to buy a football.

7. The pilot is _____ around the world.

8. Three _____ by two equals six.

9. The trees were _____ in the breeze.

10. Using binoculars, we _____ on the robbers.

Spelling and Writing

Proofreading

Proofreading Marks

○ spelling mistake

⊙ add period

Each sentence below has two mistakes. Use the proofreading marks to fix each mistake. Write the misspelled **list words** correctly on the lines.

1. Teddy Roosevelt was a president who studied the environment

2. He wooried about what was happening to the wild lands in our country

3. He helpet save the forests and wildlife

4. Most people tainked him for what he did

1. _____ 2. _____

3. _____ 4. _____

Writing a Story

Have you ever been on a camping trip or wondered what it would be like? Write a story about a camping trip you've taken or would like to take. Use as many **list words** as you can. Be sure to proofread your story. Fix any mistakes.

_____

_____

_____

_____

_____

BONUS WORDS

tossed

scolding

frying

satisfied

magnified

In lessons 19 through 23, you learned to spell words with vowels and **r**. You also learned how to form regular and irregular plurals and how to add endings to base words.

Check Your Spelling Notebook

Look at the words in your spelling notebook. Which words for lessons 19 through 23 did you have trouble with? Write them here.

_____

_____

Practice writing your troublesome words with a partner. Form the letters of each word using clay. Your partner can spell the words aloud as you form the letters.

Lesson 19

 The letter **r** can change the sound of a vowel in a word. Listen for the vowel sounds in <u>party</u>, <u>fork</u>, <u>year</u>, and <u>care</u>.

List Words

large
start
before
garden
morning
clear
appear

Write a **list word** that means the opposite of each word given. One of the words will not be used.

1. after _____

2. small _____

3. vanish _____

4. finish _____

5. muddy _____

6. evening _____

TIP The **ur** sound you hear in <u>hurt</u> can be spelled with **ir, or, er, ear, ar,** or **ur**.

Write each **list word** under the number of syllables it contains.

List Words

early

first

honor

sugar

earth

learn

one syllable	two syllables
1. _____	4. _____
2. _____	5. _____
3. _____	6. _____

Lesson 21

 TIP Add **s** to most nouns to make them plural, as in <u>hunters</u>. If a noun ends in **x, s, sh,** or **ch**, add **es** to make it plural, as in <u>bunches</u>. If a noun ends in a consonant and **y**, change the **y** to **i** and add **es**, as in <u>berries</u>.

Write the **list words** in alphabetical order.

List Words

inches

desks

watches

bushes

puppies

babies

1. _____	4. _____
2. _____	5. _____
3. _____	6. _____

If a word ends in **f** or **fe**, usually change the **f** or **fe** to **v** and add **es**, as in <u>leaves</u>. Some words change their spellings to make the plural form, as in <u>men</u>. Others have the same form for singular and plural, as in <u>deer</u>.

List Words

children
geese
sheep
wolves
heroes
women

Write each **list word** under the correct heading.

animals	people
1. _____	4. _____
2. _____	5. _____
3. _____	6. _____

Lesson 23

 Base words often change their spellings when an ending is added. For a word ending with a vowel and **y**, add only the ending, as in <u>prayed</u>. For a word ending with a consonant and **y**, change the **y** to **i** before adding the ending, unless the ending begins with **i**, as in <u>married</u> and <u>marrying</u>.

List Words

rained
studied
worried
copying
hurried
flying
replied

Write a **list word** that matches each clue. One word will not be used.

1. went faster   _____

2. answered the question   _____

3. made the day wet   _____

4. did schoolwork   _____

5. doing the same thing again   _____

6. bothered   _____

Show What You Know

One word is misspelled in each set of **list words**. Fill in the circle next to the **list word** that is spelled incorrectly.

1. ○ spyed ○ brushes ○ first ○ camping ○ appear
2. ○ compare ○ thanked ○ coorse ○ children ○ potatoes
3. ○ teeth ○ garden ○ dishes ○ shugar ○ trying
4. ○ bushes ○ helped ○ studied ○ takses ○ sheep
5. ○ phork ○ early ○ care ○ nurse ○ desks
6. ○ worried ○ paper ○ cattle ○ branches ○ wifes
7. ○ peaches ○ multiplied ○ start ○ lurn ○ leaves
8. ○ marryed ○ world ○ watches ○ morning ○ oxen
9. ○ prayed ○ babies ○ min ○ copying ○ worrying
10. ○ bunches ○ passses ○ Saturday ○ dressing ○ swaying
11. ○ large ○ acted ○ myce ○ worse ○ inches
12. ○ women ○ befor ○ hobbies ○ honor ○ fish
13. ○ wurkbook ○ chair ○ puppies ○ cleaning ○ loaves
14. ○ shelves ○ classes ○ year ○ repairing ○ raind
15. ○ deer ○ ferless ○ hurried ○ third ○ cones
16. ○ geese ○ farmer ○ boxes ○ pour ○ hunturs
17. ○ cheer ○ glasses ○ service ○ woolves ○ replied
18. ○ curly ○ order ○ knives ○ berryz ○ purse
19. ○ heroes ○ lives ○ party ○ hert ○ clear
20. ○ court ○ better ○ earth ○ flyng ○ prepare

Spelling Words in Action

What does it take to be a champion swimmer?

✎ Golden Girl ✎

Jenny Thompson is an Olympic **swimmer**. She is the **winner** of eight gold medals. Jenny finished in first place in eight Olympic relay races. She has also won 23 national awards, making her one of the **biggest** medal winners in the world!

In 1994, Jenny and her friend were playing on a water slide. Jenny **slipped** and broke her arm. The doctors said that her swimming season would have to be **stopped**. Jenny **admitted** that swimming was very important to her, and she was very determined. Two weeks later, after having seven screws and a metal plate put into her arm, Jenny won the race at the national championships!

When Jenny was just **beginning** at the age of seven, she joined a swim club. That was the first **stepping** stone on the road to the Olympics. Her coach watched her as she **skimmed** across the water with ease. He **bragged** that she could someday become a great swimmer. He was right!

Look back at the words in dark print. What do you notice about the spellings of the base words when the endings are added?

101

TIP

When a short-vowel word ends with one consonant, double the consonant before adding an ending that begins with a vowel.

swim + **er** = swimmer
cut + **ing** = cutting

Do not double the final **x** in base words ending in **x**.

flex + **ing** = flexing
fax + **ed** = faxed

Spelling Practice

LIST WORDS

1. swimmer *swimmer*
2. biggest *biggest*
3. winner *winner*
4. cutting *cutting*
5. faxed *faxed*
6. setting *setting*
7. stopped *stopped*
8. wetter *wetter*
9. slipped *slipped*
10. stepping *stepping*
11. beginning *beginning*
12. admitted *admitted*
13. jogger *jogger*
14. flexing *flexing*
15. waxed *waxed*
16. bragged *bragged*
17. trapped *trapped*
18. skimmed *skimmed*
19. trimming *trimming*
20. shipped *shipped*

Adding Endings

Write each **list word** under the correct heading. Circle the ending in each **list word**.

the final consonant is not doubled before an ending is added

1. _____ 2. _____
3. _____

the final consonant is doubled before **ed** is added

4. _____ 5. _____
6. _____ 7. _____
8. _____ 9. _____
10. _____

the final consonant is doubled before **ing** is added

11. _____ 12. _____
13. _____ 14. _____
15. _____

the final consonant is doubled before **er** is added

16. _____ 17. _____
18. _____ 19. _____

the final consonant is doubled before **est** is added

20. _____

102   Lesson 25 • Endings Added to Base Words

Word Meaning

Write the **list word** whose meaning matches each clue. Then, read down the shaded boxes to answer the riddle.

1. largest

2. one who runs slowly

3. said to be true

4. dividing into parts

5. one who moves in water

6. walking

7. polished

8. bending or tightening your muscles

Riddle: What does a boat eat for breakfast?

Answer: ___ ___ ___ ___ ___ ___ ___ ___

Endings

Make a **list word** from the underlined base word in each sentence. Write the **list words** on the lines.

1. Since it was raining harder, the streets were <u>wet</u>. _____

2. We <u>slip</u> on the icy sidewalk. _____

3. The children had more energy at the <u>begin</u> of the day. _____

4. The <u>win</u> got a gold medal. _____

5. The car <u>stop</u> at the red light. _____

6. The dog was <u>step</u> on the grass. _____

7. We <u>fax</u> the letter to the office. _____

8. Can you have the box <u>ship</u>? _____

9. Dad <u>brag</u> about the good job I had done. _____

10. The mouse was <u>trap</u> by the large cat. _____

11. Today we will be <u>trim</u> the lawn. _____

Spelling and Writing

Proofreading

Each sentence below has two mistakes. Use the proofreading marks to fix each mistake. Write the misspelled **list words** correctly on the lines.

1. In the beeginning, the Olympic games were held in greece.

2. today, the seting of the Olympics changes each time they are held.

3. Some cities have never stopt wanting to host the games

4. it would probably be the bigest event the city ever had.

5. Maybe one day your town will have the top swimar in the Olympics

1. _____

2. _____

3. _____

4. _____

5. _____

Writing a Narrative Paragraph

What is your favorite sport? Write a paragraph that tells about the sport you like best and why. Use as many **list words** as you can. Remember to proofread your paragraph. Fix any mistakes.

_____

_____

_____

_____

_____

Bonus Words

stirred

dimmer

clapping

splitting

maddest

Spelling Words in Action

What are many people afraid to do?

Speak Up!

What happens when the **teacher** calls on you? Do your mouth and **throat** get dry? Do you start to shake and forget everything you know? If so, you are not alone. Many people feel the same way.

A **group** of scientists asked people what things make them afraid. Some people **said** that they are afraid of bugs. Others said they are afraid of being in high places. Many people said they **feel** most afraid to **speak** in public.

Is speaking in front of your class one of your great fears? If so, here are some tips that will help you:

1. Be prepared. If you are **ready**, you will know what to say or have a good answer.
2. Be proud. You have something important to say.
3. Remember that you are not alone. **Sooner** or later, everyone gets called on. Your classmates don't want you to **fail**, because they don't want to fail either.
4. Last but not least, speak up! Take a deep breath. Clear your throat.

Say each word in dark print in the selection. Each word has two vowels that come together. What sounds do the vowel pairs make in the words?

105

TIP

In a **vowel pair**, the first vowel usually stands for the long-vowel sound and the second vowel is silent. You hear the long **e** in <u>teacher</u> and the long **a** in <u>fail</u>.

In a **vowel digraph**, two vowels together can make a long-vowel sound, a short-vowel sound, or a special sound all their own, as in <u>said</u>, <u>ready</u>, and <u>group</u>, and <u>sooner</u>.

Spelling Practice

Vowel Pairs and Digraphs

Write each **list word** under the correct heading.

vowel pairs with the long **a** sound

1. _____ 2. _____

vowel pairs with the long **e** sound

3. _____ 4. _____

5. _____ 6. _____

7. _____ 8. _____

9. _____ 10. _____

vowel pairs with the long **o** sound

11. _____ 12. _____

13. _____

vowel pairs with the long **i** sound

14. _____

vowel digraphs

15. _____ 16. _____

17. _____ 18. _____

19. _____ 20. _____

LIST WORDS

1. teacher *teacher*
2. feel *feel*
3. speak *speak*
4. clue *clue*
5. fail *fail*
6. soak *soak*
7. below *below*
8. lie *lie*
9. needle *needle*
10. said *said*
11. group *group*
12. feast *feast*
13. ready *ready*
14. cheap *cheap*
15. again *again*
16. throat *throat*
17. eager *eager*
18. sooner *sooner*
19. least *least*
20. contain *contain*

Classification

Write the **list word** that belongs in each group.

1. touch, taste, _____

2. anxious, willing, _____

3. spoke, talked, _____

4. wash, scrub, _____

5. hint, suggestion, _____

6. sit, stand, _____

7. neck, mouth, _____

8. crowd, gang, _____

9. principal, student, _____

10. under, beneath, _____

Definitions

Write the **list word** that matches each meaning. Use the number code to answer the riddle. Find the letter with the number 1 below it. Write that letter on each line with the number 1 under it. Do the same for the other numbers.

1. a person who works at a school ___ ___ ___ ___ ___ ___ ___
                                                8   1   2

2. not to win or succeed ___ ___ ___ ___
                         6

3. smallest in size or amount ___ ___ ___ ___ ___
                            3   4

4. to say, tell, whisper, or shout ___ ___ ___ ___
                              7   5

Riddle: What did the goat have when it ate a dollar bill?

Answer: It had a ___ ___ ___ ___ ___   ___ ___ ___ ___ ___!
                     1   2   3   4   5   6   3   4   7   8

Spelling and Writing

Proofreading

The diary entry below has ten mistakes. Use the proofreading marks to fix the mistakes. Write the misspelled **list words** correctly on the lines.

september 12, 2002

   Am I glad this day is over! today, my teecher asked me to speke in front of the class. When she called my name, I started to fele nervous. Then, my throet felt like it was closing up, and my legs started to shake. Finally, I sed to myself, "the souner I get started, the sooner I'll be done." Now that it's all over, I'm not not quite sure why I was so nervous. It really wasn't too bad.

1. _____

2. _____

3. _____

4. _____

5. _____

6. _____

Writing a Paragraph

Have you ever had to give a book report or read or speak in front of a group of people? How did it make you feel? Use the **list words** to write a paragraph about sharing your feelings. Be sure to proofread your paragraph. Fix any mistakes.

_____

_____

_____

_____

_____

BONUS WORDS

bouquet

beneath

steady

stain

mood

Spelling Words in Action

What does SPF mean?

Save Your Skin!

Did you know that the sun can damage your skin? The sun's ultraviolet rays cause sunburn, which can harm, dry, and age your skin. Also, heat can cause sunstroke. If you follow these safety tips, however, you won't have to say **goodbye** to the sun.

- Avoid direct sunlight, especially at midday. The sun's rays are the strongest in the late morning or early **afternoon**. It doesn't mean that you have to keep away from the **brook**, beach, or **pool**. Just stay in a shady spot. It's **cooler** in the shade!
- Wear a big, **loose**-fitting hat, or bring an umbrella.
- Use sunscreen. **Choose** one that has a high SPF. SPF means sun protection factor. Experts recommend using an SPF of 15 or higher.
- If you do get burned, **soothe** the ache with aloe cream.

For **goodness'** sake, keep cool. A big **scoop** of frozen yogurt can always help beat the heat.

Look back at the words in dark print. Notice that each word has the vowel digraph <u>oo</u>. Say each word. How many different vowel sounds do you hear?

TIP

The vowels **oo** together stand for three different sounds.

You can hear the different sounds in the words <u>cooler</u>, <u>brook</u>, and <u>blood</u>. Listen for the sound the vowels **oo** stand for in each **list word**.

Spelling Practice

LIST WORDS

1. scoop *scoop*
2. shoot *shoot*
3. afternoon *afternoon*
4. cooler *cooler*
5. roof *roof*
6. broom *broom*
7. pool *pool*
8. choose *choose*
9. goose *goose*
10. soothe *soothe*
11. loose *loose*
12. stood *stood*
13. goodness *goodness*
14. wool *wool*
15. brook *brook*
16. cookie *cookie*
17. goodbye *goodbye*
18. wooden *wooden*
19. soot *soot*
20. blood *blood*

Words with oo

Write each **list word** under the correct heading.

oo as in <u>cool</u>

1. _____
2. _____
3. _____
4. _____
5. _____
6. _____
7. _____
8. _____
9. _____
10. _____
11. _____

oo as in <u>book</u>

12. _____
13. _____
14. _____
15. _____
16. _____
17. _____
18. _____
19. _____

oo as in <u>flood</u>

20. _____

Scrambled Crossword

Unscramble the letters to form **list words**.
Print one letter in each box to complete
the puzzle.

ACROSS

2. kooice
4. owoned
6. tosoh
8. esotoh
9. dlobo
10. loow

DOWN

1. doogenss
2. loocer
3. sooge
5. doots
7. loop
9. okobr

Comparing Words

Read the first two underlined words in each sentence. Write the **list word** that
goes with the third word in the same way.

1. come is to leave as hello is to _____

2. before 12 is to after 12 as morning is to _____

3. snow is to shovel as dust is to _____

4. head is to hat as building is to _____

5. fireplace is to ash as chimney is to _____

6. lake is to pond as river is to _____

7. pie is to tart as cake is to _____

8. dart is to throw as arrow is to _____

9. skate is to rink as swim is to _____

10. drake is to duck as gander is to _____

Spelling and Writing

Proofreading

The recipe below has nine mistakes. Use the proofreading marks to fix the mistakes. Write the misspelled **list words** correctly on the lines.

Summer Salad

Here's a recipe that will make a warm summer afternun just a little bit couler.

- First, chooz your favorite kinds of melons. watermelon, Honeydew, and cantaloupe are the best.
- next, cut them in half and scoope out the insides.
- Then, use the Hollowed-out skin of one of the melons as a bowl for the melon balls.
- finally, enjoy!

1. _____

2. _____

3. _____

4. _____

Writing an Advertisement

The danger of ultraviolet rays makes sunscreen important for everyone. Use the **list words** to write a persuasive ad that will convince people to use sunscreen. Be sure to proofread your sunscreen ad. Fix any mistakes.

_____

_____

_____

_____

BONUS WORDS

bamboo

flood

raccoon

crooked

gloomy

Spelling Words in Action

Why do fireflies glow?

Buggy Lights

Have you ever been traveling at **night** on a **highway** and seen dozens of tiny **bright** lights glowing in the darkness? Of course, mostly everyone knows that those little twinkles are fireflies. They are also called lightning bugs. These flickering creatures are really not flies at all. They are beetles.

Scientists are not really sure why fireflies glow. Their flashing may be a way for them to communicate to one another. It is also **thought** that the bugs are sending off **light** as a signal to other animals that **would** like to eat them. Scientists believe it's as if the bugs **might** be saying, "Don't eat me! I have glowing chemicals in my body, and I taste awful!"

Fireflies are actually quite harmless. They don't bite. They don't even have pincers. They can't even fly very fast. In fact, they are so slow, that you can easily catch them in your hands.

In many places the **sight** of fireflies twinkling in the **moonlight** is a sure sign of summer.

Say each word in dark print in the selection. Which letters do not make a sound?

Spelling Practice

TIP

In each **list word**, you will find that **gh** or **l** is not heard. Look for these spelling patterns in your **list words**:

al as in <u>calf</u>

igh as in <u>light</u>

oul as in <u>would</u>

eigh as in <u>eight</u>

ough as in <u>through</u>

ough as in <u>fought</u>

LIST WORDS

1. fight   *fight*
2. half   *half*
3. sight   *sight*
4. would   *would*
5. night   *night*
6. light   *light*
7. calf   *calf*
8. might   *might*
9. highway   *highway*
10. moonlight *moonlight*
11. bright   *bright*
12. eight   *eight*
13. thought   *thought*
14. through   *through*
15. weight   *weight*
16. fright   *fright*
17. sigh   *sigh*
18. slight   *slight*
19. fought   *fought*
20. knight   *knight*

Words with Silent gh and l

Write each **list word** under the correct heading. Circle the silent consonant or consonants in each word.

igh as in <u>bright</u>   **al** as in <u>calf</u>

1. _____   13. _____

2. _____   14. _____

3. _____

                          oul as is <u>could</u>

4. _____   15. _____

5. _____

                          eigh as in <u>freight</u>

6. _____   16. _____

7. _____   17. _____

8. _____

                          ough as in <u>through</u>

9. _____   18. _____

10. _____

                          ough as in <u>brought</u>

11. _____   19. _____

12. _____   20. _____

Dictionary

Write the **list word** for each sound-spelling given.

In a dictionary, a **sound-spelling** appears after each entry word. It tells how to pronounce the word, as in **weight** (wāt).

1. (sīt) _____

2. (nīt) _____

3. (wŏŏd) _____

4. (mīt) _____

5. (slīt) _____   8. (sī) _____

6. (fôt) _____   9. (wāt) _____

7. (mōōn′ līt) _____   10. (līt) _____

Puzzle

Write the **list word** whose meaning matches each clue.

ACROSS
2. in and out
7. a main road
8. battle
9. scared

DOWN
1. before nine
2. idea
3. glowing
4. not whole
5. soldier who wore armor
6. baby cow

Spelling and Writing

Proofreading

Proofreading Marks

⬭ spelling mistake

≡ capital letter

⊙ add period

There are two mistakes in each sentence below. Use the proofreading marks to fix each mistake. Rewrite the misspelled **list words** correctly on the lines.

1. Last nite in the moonlite, we collected fireflies.

2. We caught aight bugs and put them in a jar

3. I thot that they might fly out thru the holes in the cap.

4. the glow from the bugs was very brite.

5. Their light was quite a site

1. _____

_____

2. _____

3. _____

_____

4. _____

5. _____

Writing a Description

Imagine that you are a firefly. Write a paragraph that describes where you live and why you glow in the dark. Try to use as many **list words** as you can. Be sure to proofread your paragraph. Fix any mistakes.

_____

_____

_____

_____

_____

BONUS WORDS

flight

behalf

freight

although

sought

Spelling Words in Action

Why was coin collecting called "the hobby of kings"?

Royal Hobby

Coin collecting was once thought to be "the hobby of kings." That's **because**, at one time, only a king could afford to keep money. Most people had to spend all their money just to live. Today, you don't have to be a king to collect coins. Over 5 million Americans across the country are doing it! Many **belong** to collecting clubs.

To begin, all you need are a few coins and a folder in which to keep them. **Almost** any hobby shop can sell you this special kind of folder. There is a pocket in the folder for each coin. You might start by saving pennies. Try to find ones with the date for each year of your life.

Look for coins without scratches. A coin without a **flaw** is worth more than others. However, it is not **all right** to clean a dirty coin. Rubbing wears down its face and makes it less valuable. Very old coins are hard to find and could **cost** a lot if you **bought** them. You could get lucky, though. You might **already** have a valuable coin right in your own pocket!

Say each word in dark print in the selection. Can you hear the ô sound as in <u>lost</u> in each word?

117

Spelling Practice

TIP

The ô sound can be spelled many ways:

au as in <u>because</u>

aw as in <u>flaw</u>

o as in <u>cost</u>

ou as in <u>bought</u>

al as in <u>already</u>

Look at the spelling of the **ô** sound in each **list word**.

LIST WORDS

1. already   *already*
2. because   *because*
3. almost   *almost*
4. flaw   *flaw*
5. cost   *cost*
6. wallet   *wallet*
7. laws   *laws*
8. lost   *lost*
9. long   *long*
10. belong   *belong*
11. across   *across*
12. all right   *all right*
13. bought   *bought*
14. August   *August*
15. chalk   *chalk*
16. haul   *haul*
17. awful   *awful*
18. crawl   *crawl*
19. lawn   *lawn*
20. caught   *caught*

Words with the ô Sound

Write each **list word** under the correct spelling of its **ô** sound.

au

1. _____
2. _____
3. _____
4. _____

aw

5. _____
6. _____
7. _____
8. _____
9. _____

al

10. _____
11. _____
12. _____
13. _____
14. _____

o or **ou**

15. _____
16. _____
17. _____
18. _____
19. _____
20. _____

Word-Shape Puzzle

Unscramble the letters to spell **list words**. Then, use the number code to answer the riddle.

1. lal ___ ___ ___
             10

2. higtr ___ ___ ___ ___ ___
             4   6

3. secabeu ___ ___ ___ ___ ___ ___ ___
                        3   11 9

4. ckalh ___ ___ ___ ___ ___
              7   8

5. fwal ___ ___ ___ ___
             1

6. nogl ___ ___ ___ ___
              2   5

Riddle: What has four heads and four tails?

Answer: ___ ___ ___ ___ ___ ___ ___ ___ ___ ___ ___
             1   2   3   4   5   6   7   8   9   10 11

Definitions

Write the **list word** that matches each meaning.

1. rules people must obey

_____

2. to be part of something

_____

3. missing

_____

4. grass

_____

5. to move like a worm

_____

6. terrible

_____

7. not quite

_____

8. to carry by wagon or truck

_____

9. the eighth month of the year

_____

10. by or before this time

_____

Spelling and Writing

Proofreading

This article has eight mistakes. Use the proofreading marks to fix each mistake. Write the misspelled **list words** correctly on the lines.

Proofreading Marks

⬭ spelling mistake

⌃ add something

℮ take out something

Collecting baseball cards is a popular hobby akross the country. Many kids are trading cards they bowght at hobby shops. Would you like to be a collector If so, remember that some some cards cawst a lot. So, be careful not to get cawt spending too much.? You'll need to keep some change in your waulet—just in case you spot the card that will complete your collection.

1. _____ 2. _____

3. _____ 4. _____

5. _____

Writing a Paragraph

People enjoy collecting many different things. Do you collect something? Write a paragraph describing your collection or something you would like to collect. Use as many **list words** as you can. Proofread your paragraph. Fix any mistakes.

BONUS WORDS

moth

sausage

awkward

altogether

brought

_____

_____

_____

_____

_____

Lesson 30

In lessons 25 through 29, you learned to spell words with vowel pairs and digraphs, and words with **oo** and the **ô** sound. You also learned to spell words with silent consonants and how to add endings to base words.

Check Your Spelling Notebook

Look at the words in your spelling notebook. Which words in lessons 25 through 29 did you have the most trouble with? Write them here.

_____

_____

Practice writing your troublesome words with a partner. Try writing the letters for each word in a tray of sand, salt, or sugar. Your partner can check your spelling as you write.

Lesson 25

 For short-vowel words that end with one consonant other than **x**, double the consonant before adding an ending that begins with a vowel, as in <u>stopped</u> and <u>cutting</u>.

Write this set of **list words** in alphabetical order. Draw a circle around each base word.

List Words

swimmer
biggest
winner
slipped
beginning
admitted

1. _____

2. _____

3. _____

4. _____

5. _____

6. _____

Most **vowel pairs** spell long-vowel sounds, as in <u>least</u>. **Vowel digraphs** can spell long- or short-vowel sounds or make a sound all their own, as in <u>said</u>, <u>ready</u>, and <u>group</u>.

List Words

group

soak

clue

speak

again

said

least

Write a **list word** that rhymes with each word given. One word will not be used.

1. fed _____

2. peek _____

3. feast _____

4. poke _____

5. loop _____

6. flew _____

 The vowel digraph **oo** can stand for three sounds, as in <u>scoop</u>, <u>soot</u>, and <u>blood</u>.

List Words

shoot

brook

choose

stood

cookie

soothe

Write each **list word** under the word with the same vowel sound.

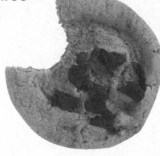

<u>scoop</u>   <u>good</u>

1. _____ 4. _____

2. _____ 5. _____

3. _____ 6. _____

TIP Some words contain silent letters, such as **l** in <u>half</u> and **gh** in <u>sight</u>.

List Words

fight
calf
eight
would
highway
fright
half

Write the **list word** that matches each clue. One word will not be used.

1. a number _____

2. argue _____

3. a kind of road _____

4. sounds like <u>wood</u> _____

5. feeling of fear _____

6. baby cow _____

TIP The sound of ô can be spelled many ways as in <u>flaw</u>, <u>because</u>, <u>already</u>, and <u>bought</u>.

List Words

lost
caught
crawl
bought
long
awful
haul

Write a **list word** that means the opposite of each word given. One word will not be used.

1. wonderful _____

2. sold _____

3. short _____

4. found _____

5. push _____

6. released _____

Show What You Know

One word is misspelled in each set of **list words**. Fill in the circle next to the **list word** that is spelled incorrectly.

1. ○ cookie ○ fite ○ already ○ needle ○ stopped
2. ○ throte ○ night ○ trapped ○ across ○ scoop
3. ○ cost ○ caught ○ chooze ○ teacher ○ swimmer
4. ○ weight ○ shipped ○ loose ○ faksed ○ below
5. ○ waxed ○ sooner ○ sut ○ lost ○ haul
6. ○ wollet ○ afternoon ○ thought ○ broom ○ fail
7. ○ almost ○ sie ○ sight ○ winner ○ feel
8. ○ all right ○ fought ○ contane ○ cheap ○ bragged
9. ○ long ○ goose ○ night ○ group ○ beggining
10. ○ caf ○ bright ○ least ○ skimmed ○ brook
11. ○ half ○ crauwl ○ bought ○ biggest ○ eager
12. ○ would ○ lawn ○ cooler ○ goodbye ○ moonlite
13. ○ awful ○ pool ○ cutting ○ slipt ○ speak
14. ○ slight ○ soak ○ trimming ○ Agust ○ stood
15. ○ light ○ roof ○ joger ○ again ○ setting
16. ○ lie ○ becos ○ blood ○ laws ○ highway
17. ○ wetter ○ soothe ○ clew ○ eight ○ flaw
18. ○ gudness ○ chalk ○ wool ○ stepping ○ said
19. ○ belong ○ shewt ○ fright ○ ready ○ admitted
20. ○ flexing ○ feest ○ wooden ○ through ○ knight

Spelling Words in Action

What is clown college?

Clowning Around

Did you ever think about how a **clown** learns to be a clown? Before running off to **join** the circus many clowns went to a special school. It was the Ringling Brothers College for Clowns. Irving Feld, the owner of Ringling Brothers Circus, started the school in 1968.

In clown college, students learned **about** tumbling, riding a unicycle, falling down and making people laugh. The students who went to clown college really got to **enjoy** themselves, but it was hard work. Each student created a special clown character. One clown may have been fat with a big, **round** face. Another may have been tall with a head that came to a **point**. Each clown had to have a different face. The **choice** of how the face looked was up to the student. When they graduated, they were **proud** of what they had done.

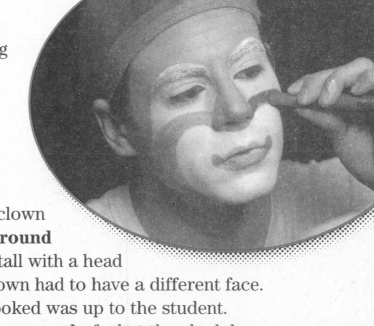

In 1998, the Ringling Brothers College for Clowns closed. It had trained 1,400 clowns. The next time the circus comes to your **town**, think of Mr. Feld when the clowns make you laugh.

Say each word in dark print in the selection.
How are the words with the <u>oi</u> sound spelled?
How are the words with the <u>ou</u> sound spelled?

TIP

The **oi** sound may be spelled **oy** as in toys or **oi** as in coin. The **ou** sound may be spelled **ow** as in town or **ou** as in proud. Each **list word** has the **oi** or **ou** sound. Look at how the sound is spelled in each word.

LIST WORDS

1. clown   *clown*
2. join   *join*
3. town   *town*
4. crowd   *crowd*
5. enjoy   *enjoy*
6. round   *round*
7. loud   *loud*
8. point   *point*
9. coin   *coin*
10. toys   *toys*
11. about   *about*
12. proud   *proud*
13. allow   *allow*
14. foil   *foil*
15. power   *power*
16. pound   *pound*
17. blouse   *blouse*
18. crown   *crown*
19. choice   *choice*
20. loyal   *loyal*

Words with the oi and ou Sounds

Write each **list word** under the correct heading.

ow as in <u>how</u>

1. _____
2. _____
3. _____
4. _____
5. _____
6. _____

ou as in <u>sound</u>

12. _____
13. _____
14. _____
15. _____
16. _____
17. _____

oi as in <u>oil</u>

7. _____
8. _____
9. _____
10. _____
11. _____

oy as in <u>boy</u>

18. _____
19. _____
20. _____

Word Building

Build **list words** by replacing letters. Write the **list words**.

1. enter – ter + joy = _____

2. voice – v + ch = _____

3. alone – one + low = _____

4. sound – s + r = _____

5. black – ack + ouse = _____

6. joint – j + p = _____

7. crown – n + d = _____

8. royal – r + l = _____

9. pouch – ch + nd = _____

10. brown – br + cl = _____

11. above – ve + ut = _____

12. coil – l + n = _____

13. boys – b + t = _____

14. jolly – lly + in = _____

Rhyming

Write a **list word** that rhymes with the underlined clue to complete each silly definition.

1. A place where funny people live is a <u>clown</u> _____.

2. A group of noisy people is a _____ <u>crowd</u>.

3. A monster who cooks and eats metal things might <u>boil</u> _____.

4. A cloud that is pleased with itself is a _____ <u>cloud</u>.

5. A sad or angry king might wear a <u>frown</u> _____.

6. A king who is true to his country

   is a _____ <u>royal</u>.

7. A king who rules from the top

   of a castle has <u>tower</u> _____.

Spelling and Writing

Proofreading

This poem has eleven mistakes. Use the proofreading marks to fix each mistake. Write the misspelled **list words** correctly on the lines.

the circus is coming to toun.
I can't wait to to see a clooun.
i've heard there will be lots of toiys
For all all the happy girls and boys.
I can't wait to joyn the the croud
And laugh and cheer and clap out lowd.

Proofreading Marks

◯ spelling mistake
≡ capital letter
℮ take out something

1. _____

2. _____

3. _____

4. _____

5. _____

6. _____

Writing a Description

If you could be a clown, what kind of clown would you be? How would you look? What would you do to make people laugh? Draw a picture of yourself as a clown. Then, use the **list words** to write a few sentences describing your act. Be sure to proofread your work. Fix any mistakes.

_____

_____

_____

_____

BONUS WORDS

avoid

doubt

destroy

spoil

drown

Spelling Words in Action

Why does a meteorite glow?

Shooting Stars?

Did you know that shooting stars aren't really stars at all? They start out as cold chunks of rock speeding through space. If one gets caught near the Earth and starts falling, it gets so hot that it glows. Scientists call this shooting star a meteor.

Most of these glowing space rocks burn up in the air and **disappear**. The very few that ever reach the Earth are called meteorites. These special rocks often go **unseen** on the ground. You would probably be **unable** to tell a meteorite from an ordinary Earth rock.

Scientists have been able to **discover** many meteorites in Antarctica, near the South Pole. The dark rocks are easy to see on the empty, **uneven** ice fields. The cold, dry air has kept many meteorites **unchanged** for thousands of years. Unlike those in other places, the meteorites in Antarctica have been **untouched** by **unclean** air and by weather.

That shooting star you see may not make your wish come true, but that doesn't mean it's **unlucky**. Scientists say it could unlock some secrets of the planets and outer space.

Look back at the words in dark print. These words have word parts, or prefixes, added to the front of them to make new words. Name the two prefixes.

TIP

A **prefix** is a word part added to the beginning of a base word. It changes the base word's meaning. The prefixes **dis** and **un** mean <u>not</u> or <u>the opposite</u>, as in <u>unseen</u> and <u>dislike</u>. Think about the meaning of each **list word**.

Spelling Practice

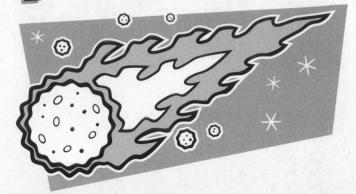

LIST WORDS

1. unseen   *unseen*
2. unable   *unable*
3. discover   *discover*
4. unload   *unload*
5. unclean   *unclean*
6. unsure   *unsure*
7. uneven   *uneven*
8. dislike   *dislike*
9. displease   *displease*
10. distrust   *distrust*
11. unwrap   *unwrap*
12. untrue   *untrue*
13. unlucky   *unlucky*
14. unchanged   *unchanged*
15. untouched   *untouched*
16. disobey   *disobey*
17. disorder   *disorder*
18. unbutton   *unbutton*
19. unpaid   *unpaid*
20. disappear   *disappear*

Words with Prefixes

Write each **list word** under the correct heading.

words with the prefix **dis**

1. _____   2. _____

3. _____   4. _____

5. _____   6. _____

7. _____

words with the prefix **un**

8. _____   9. _____

10. _____ 11. _____

12. _____ 13. _____

14. _____ 15. _____

16. _____ 17. _____

18. _____ 19. _____

20. _____

Synonyms

Write the **list word** that means the same as the word given.

1. find _____

2. hate _____

3. false _____

4. dirty _____

5. mess _____

6. annoy _____

7. vanish _____

8. uncertain _____

Scrambled Letters

Unscramble the letters to spell each base word. Then, add the prefix **un** or **dis** to make a **list word**.

1. doutech _____

2. aldo _____

3. praw _____

4. hangced _____

5. boye _____

6. neev _____

7. surtt _____

8. tunobt _____

9. nese _____

10. apid _____

11. culky _____

12. bale _____

13. nalec _____

14. rocev _____

15. retu _____

16. dorer _____

17. leapse _____

18. rapepa _____

19. ruse _____

20. eikl _____

Spelling and Writing

Proofreading

This diary entry has nine mistakes. Use the proofreading marks to fix the mistakes. Write the misspelled **list words** correctly on the lines.

Proofreading Marks

○ spelling mistake

≡ capital letter

↘ add apostrophe

April 4

    last night, I was unabel to sleep so I got up and watched the stars. Suddenly, I saw something streak through the sky and then disappeer. I was surprised and a little unshure of what Id seen. So, I listened to the news this morning hoping to diskover the answer. sure enough, the news reported the sighting of a meteor last night. what a relief! Now I know I wasnt seeing things.

1. _____ 2. _____

3. _____ 4. _____

Writing Sentences

Have you ever wished on a star? What did you wish for? Write a few sentences telling about your wish. Use as many **list words** as you can. Be sure to proofread your sentences. Fix any mistakes.

_____

_____

_____

_____

_____

BONUS WORDS

unusual

uneasy

unprepared

disrespect

distaste

Spelling Words in Action

Why did it take so long for Bartholdi to finish his statue?

Bigger Than Life

In New York Harbor, she stands more than twenty-times larger than life. One finger is taller than a person. Her full name is "Liberty Enlightening the World." We often **rename** her the Statue of Liberty.

This **lovely** statue was a gift to the United States from France. In the 1700s, both countries had fought for freedom. The French people were **hoping** to **remind** Americans of the friendship and freedom they were now **sharing**.

The artist, Frederic Auguste Bartholdi, took nearly ten years to finish the statue. He began by **making** a small clay model. Then, he built a larger one out of copper. He marked it off into 300 pieces. Each piece was then made in an even larger size. He shipped the pieces to America so that his workers could **rebuild** it. In 1886, on an island in New York Harbor, the giant puzzle was finally put together.

Today, Lady Liberty stands proudly holding her torch. No other statue could ever **replace** her.

Take a look at the words in dark print in the selection. What prefixes, endings, and suffixes can you identify?

133

TIP

If a word ends in a silent **e**, drop the **e** before adding an ending that begins with a vowel.

share + ing = <u>sharing</u>

Keep the final **e** when a suffix begins with a consonant.

love + ly = <u>lovely</u>

The prefix **re** can mean again or back.

re + <u>build</u> = <u>rebuild</u>, meaning build again

Spelling Practice

LIST WORDS

1. rename *rename*
2. remind *remind*
3. sharing *sharing*
4. hoping *hoping*
5. rewrite *rewrite*
6. making *making*
7. lately *lately*
8. dancing *dancing*
9. reload *reload*
10. serving *serving*
11. replace *replace*
12. lovely *lovely*
13. racing *racing*
14. closely *closely*
15. rebuild *rebuild*
16. recopy *recopy*
17. regroup *regroup*
18. rethink *rethink*
19. politely *politely*
20. nicely *nicely*

Adding Prefixes, Endings, Suffixes

Add the prefix **re** to each of the base words to form a **list word**.

1. build _____
2. group _____
3. load _____
4. write _____
5. mind _____
6. copy _____
7. place _____
8. name _____
9. think _____

Add the suffix **ly** to each of the base words to form a **list word**.

10. late _____
11. polite _____
12. love _____
13. nice _____
14. close _____

Add the ending **ing** to each of the base words to form a **list word**.

15. share _____
16. hope _____
17. make _____
18. dance _____
19. serve _____
20. race _____

Rhyming

The base of a **list word** rhymes with each of these words. Write the complete **list word**.

1. care _____
2. dove _____
3. prance _____
4. toad _____
5. fake _____
6. pace _____
7. rope _____
8. nerve _____
9. blame _____
10. loop _____

Puzzle

Write the **list word** whose meaning matches each clue.

ACROSS
1. pleasantly
5. copy over
7. write again
9. showing good manners
10. speeding

DOWN
2. nearly
3. build again
4. not long ago
6. think again
8. help remember

Spelling and Writing

Proofreading

This article has seven mistakes. Use the proofreading marks to fix the mistakes. Write the misspelled **list words** correctly on the lines.

Can a mountain be made into a Monument Of course it can Mount Rushmore, on which the faces of four American presidents are carved, should reemind you of that fact. Nearby, another mountain will someday tell us the story of Crazy Horse, a Sioux warrior. The image of this famous warrior and his horse will eventually replase an ordinary mountain. Unfortunately, the Artist died before he could complete his sculpture. The artist's wife and family are hooping to complete this incredible work of art.

1. _____

2. _____

3. _____

Writing a Report

There are many monuments and statues that honor people or events in our history. Write a short report about one you have visited or know about. Use as many **list words** as you can. Be sure to proofread your report. Fix any mistakes.

_____

_____

_____

_____

_____

_____

reappear

servicing

redesign

losing

reorder

Spelling Words in Action

Why shouldn't you invite a bear to a picnic?

Uninvited Guests

My grandfather told me a story about a camping trip he took a few years ago. They were in Yellowstone National Park and had a visitor who **wasn't** invited. It was a yearling grizzly bear. A yearling is a grizzly **that's** about one year old. This youngster, who **couldn't** have weighed less than 150 pounds, walked into the picnic area and calmly roamed from table to table enjoying the feast. Of course, the terrified campers **didn't** stay around to watch.

The park rangers arrived, captured him, and took him to another area of the park. They moved him far enough away so that he **wouldn't** be able to come back. Grandfather said it is the park's policy to relocate bears, so that they **won't** become dependent on human food. Of course, people **mustn't** ever feed wild animals. Rangers try to keep human contact to a minimum, so that bears will stay away from the things they **shouldn't** eat.

The ranger thought that the bear might return. He claimed that bears never forget where **there's** a good meal, and this one was the best that the bear has ever had.

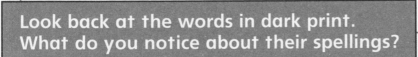

Look back at the words in dark print.
What do you notice about their spellings?

137

TIP

A **contraction** is a short way to write two words. Use an apostrophe (') to show where letters have been left out of a contraction.

I'd is a contraction for I would.

He's is a contraction for he is.

Spelling Practice

LIST WORDS

1. there's   *there's*
2. haven't   *haven't*
3. he's   *he's*
4. couldn't   *couldn't*
5. that's   *that's*
6. I'll   *I'll*
7. isn't   *isn't*
8. didn't   *didn't*
9. they're   *they're*
10. we'll   *we'll*
11. mustn't   *mustn't*
12. shouldn't   *shouldn't*
13. wasn't   *wasn't*
14. won't   *won't*
15. I'd   *I'd*
16. wouldn't   *wouldn't*
17. don't   *don't*
18. I've   *I've*
19. you've   *you've*
20. doesn't   *doesn't*

Writing Contractions

Write the **list words** under each category. Remember to include the apostrophe in each word.

the contractions that mean "**not**"

1. _____   2. _____
3. _____   4. _____
5. _____   6. _____
7. _____   8. _____
9. _____   10. _____
11. _____

the contractions that mean "**is**"

12. _____   13. _____
14. _____

the contractions that mean "**will**"

15. _____   16. _____

the contractions that mean "**have**"

17. _____   18. _____

the contraction that means "**would**"

19. _____

the contraction that has the meaning "**are**"

20. _____

Contractions

Circle the two words in each sentence that can be shortened into a contraction to make a **list word**. Then, write the **list words**.

1. You must not tell my secret. _____

2. We have not seen Bill all day. _____

3. The dog would not sit in the pond. _____

4. You have made me very happy. _____

5. I would like to find my coat. _____

6. They are all going to the party. _____

7. You should not ride your bike after dark. _____

8. I will go get the groceries. _____

9. Anne did not hear the telephone ringing. _____

10. The boys could not fix the flat tire. _____

Scrambled Words

Unscramble the letters and add an apostrophe to form **list words**. Then, use the number code to answer the riddle.

1. lelw ___ ___ ___ ___
       1

2. taths ___ ___ ___ ___ ___
        2   10

3. vie ___ ___ ___
      3

4. twon ___ ___ ___ ___
        4

5. tond ___ ___ ___ ___
     5

6. nestdo ___ ___ ___ ___ ___ ___
        6

7. stanw ___ ___ ___ ___ ___
      7

8. esh ___ ___ ___
      8

9. resthe ___ ___ ___ ___ ___ ___
       9

10. snit ___ ___ ___ ___
       11

Riddle: What did the bear say to the campers at their picnic?

Answer: ___ ___ ___ ___ ___ ___ ___ ___ ___ ___ ___?
    1 2 3 4   5 6   7 8   9 10 11

Spelling and Writing

Proofreading

Proofreading Marks

ˇ add apostrophe

e take out something

This poem has eight mistakes. Use the proofreading marks to fix each mistake. Underline the **list words**, then write them correctly on the lines.

Theres a bear in in the woods I know for sure.

Hes black and covered with fuzzy fur.

Youve never seen such a great, big beast.

Id say he is ten feet at at least.

Now I think that bear is is chasing me.

So Ill have to run and climb a tree.

1. _____

2. _____

3. _____

4. _____

5. _____

Writing a Story

Imagine that you are the bear at the picnic area. Write a paragraph telling your side of the story. Use as many **list words** as you can. Be sure to proofread your paragraph. Fix any mistakes.

_____

_____

_____

_____

_____

_____

_____

BONUS WORDS

hasn't

they'll

where's

how's

would've

Spelling Words in Action

Why is the knot called the "Hunter's Bend"?

New Knot

You're going **to hear** about a **great** new knot. It was invented in England by Dr. Edward Hunter. Some time ago, he was playing with some string and **tied** it by accident.

"I put **two** ends opposite each other," he said. "I made a **pair** of loops on each end and pulled them through one another. It was very even and easy to tie." This new knot had a shape all its own. It was quite strong and very useful. It could be used on both land and sea.

The doctor thought someone else must have **made** such a knot before. However, after many years of research, he could not find any knot like his. Finally, he took his knot to the Maritime Museum in London. There, he found books filled with pictures of far **too** many knots to count. A researcher helped him look back over 300 years of sailors' knots. They couldn't find any knots exactly like Dr. Hunter's. In fact, no one anywhere seemed to know of a knot like his.

Now it's official, Dr. Hunter has added a new knot to the books. The name of course, is "Hunter's Bend," after its inventor. It looks like Hunter has things all tied up!

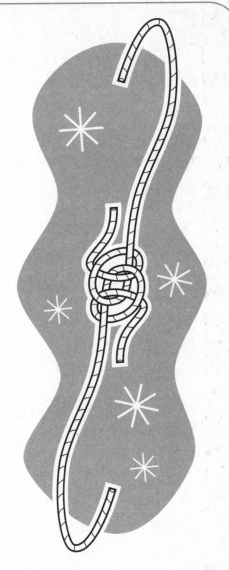

Look back at the words in dark print. Which words sound the same but have different spellings? Which words sound the same as <u>pear</u>, <u>here</u>, <u>grate</u>, <u>tide</u>, and <u>maid</u>?

Spelling Practice

LIST WORDS

1. hear   *hear*
2. here   *here*
3. tied   *tied*
4. tide   *tide*
5. your   *your*
6. you're   *you're*
7. hour   *hour*
8. our   *our*
9. sail   *sail*
10. sale   *sale*
11. two   *two*
12. too   *too*
13. to   *to*
14. pair   *pair*
15. pear   *pear*
16. pare   *pare*
17. maid   *maid*
18. made   *made*
19. great   *great*
20. grate   *grate*

Homonyms

Write the **list words** that contain the vowel sounds given.

long **a** as in <u>say</u>

1. _____
2. _____
3. _____
4. _____
5. _____
6. _____

ir sound as in <u>year</u>

7. _____
8. _____

oo sound as in <u>food</u>

9. _____
10. _____
11. _____

er sound as in <u>care</u>

12. _____
13. _____
14. _____

or sound as in <u>for</u>

15. _____
16. _____

long **i** as in <u>side</u>

17. _____
18. _____

ou sound as in <u>found</u>

19. _____
20. _____

Definitions

Write the **list word** that matches each meaning.

1. also _____
2. big _____
3. cut or trim _____
4. sixty minutes _____
5. a sea change _____
6. twins _____
7. knotted _____
8. low prices _____
9. use ears _____
10. a contraction _____
11. boat part _____
12. house cleaner _____
13. a fruit _____
14. a number _____
15. metal frame _____
16. toward _____
17. in this place _____
18. built _____

Homonyms

Write two **list words** that are homonyms to answer each riddle.

1. What did the boy say when he saw the fireplace grill?

"What a _____ _____!"

2. What did the girl ask the cook to do?

"Please _____ the skin off this _____."

3. What happened to the messy bed in the hotel room?

The _____ _____ it.

4. What did the people sitting at the concert say?

"We can really _____ well _____."

Spelling and Writing

Proofreading

This movie poster has eleven mistakes. Use the proofreading marks to fix each mistake. Circle the **list words** that are used incorrectly. Then, write the correct **list words** on the lines.

You wont want to miss hour grate new movie called *Sea Voyage*. Itll have you and you're friends on the edge of your seats. It begins when friends go go for a sale in their new boat. Their trip, which was to only last an our, takes a sudden turn when the tied takes them them far out to sea. After being lost for too weeks, they finally make it back home.

1. _____

2. _____

3. _____

4. _____

5. _____

6. _____

7. _____

Writing a Journal Entry

Imagine that you are a sailor in a boat on the open sea. Write a journal entry about your journey. Use as many **list words** as you can. Be sure to proofread your journal entry. Fix any mistakes.

_____

_____

_____

_____

_____

_____

BONUS WORDS

cent

sent

scent

blue

blew

In lessons 31 through 35, you learned to spell homonyms and contractions and words with vowel sounds **oi** and **ou**. You also learned more prefixes, endings, and suffixes to add to base words.

Check Your Spelling Notebook

Look at the words in your spelling notebook. Which words in lessons 31 through 35 gave you trouble? Write them here.

_____

_____

_____

Practice writing your troublesome words with a partner. Take turns dividing the words into syllables as your partner spells them aloud.

Lesson 31

 Listen for the **oi** sound in <u>join</u> and <u>toys</u>, and for the **ou** sound in <u>loud</u> and <u>town</u>.

Write each **list word** under the correct heading.

List Words

crowd
point
about
power
choice
loyal

one syllable	two syllables
1. _____	4. _____
2. _____	5. _____
3. _____	6. _____

A **prefix** is a word part that is added to the beginning of a base word, as in <u>unable</u> and <u>discover</u>.

List Words

distrust
unsure
untrue
displease
unlucky
disobey

Add a prefix to each word to make a **list word**. Write the **list word** on the line.

1. true _____

2. obey _____

3. please _____

4. lucky _____

5. sure _____

6. trust _____

 The prefix **re** can mean again or back, as in <u>remind</u> and <u>rewrite</u>. If a word ends with a silent **e**, drop the **e** before adding an ending that begins with a vowel. Keep the final **e** when a suffix begins with a consonant.

List Words

lately
closely
reload
politely
recopy
lovely

Write the **list words** in alphabetical order.

1. _____

2. _____

3. _____

4. _____

5. _____

6. _____

 A **contraction** is a word made by writing two words together and leaving out one or more letters. An apostrophe shows where letters are missing, as in I'll.

Write a **list word** that rhymes with each word given.

List Words

there's
couldn't
doesn't
he's
they're
I'd

1. wasn't _____

2. bears _____

3. hair _____

4. wide _____

5. bees _____

6. wouldn't _____

 Homonyms are words that sound alike, but have different meanings and spellings, such as sale and sail.

Write a **list word** to complete each sentence.

List Words

your
to
here
you're
too
hear

1. When you whisper, I can't _____ you.

2. Each person must walk _____ the exit.

3. It is getting _____ dark to read.

4. Please hang _____ coat in the hall.

5. We will be _____ when you return.

6. I see that _____ on my bus, too.

Show What You Know

One word is misspelled in each set of **list words**. Fill in the circle next to the **list word** that is spelled incorrectly.

1. ○ wouldn't ○ pound ○ pare ○ unclean ○ riplace
2. ○ uneven ○ loud ○ don't ○ sale ○ musn't
3. ○ tied ○ proud ○ rename ○ unbuton ○ there's
4. ○ unseen ○ doesn't ○ choyce ○ that's ○ grate
5. ○ rethink ○ discuver ○ I'll ○ clown ○ our
6. ○ unlucky ○ enjoy ○ youer ○ they're ○ you're
7. ○ isn't ○ town ○ maid ○ rewrite ○ dusplease
8. ○ unwrap ○ wasn't ○ sail ○ dansing ○ blouse
9. ○ coudn't ○ unsure ○ join ○ making ○ hear
10. ○ unable ○ allow ○ wan't ○ too ○ haven't
11. ○ coin ○ lovely ○ disorder ○ rimind ○ tide
12. ○ dislike ○ disappear ○ round ○ made ○ rebild
13. ○ point ○ unpaid ○ reload ○ two ○ heer
14. ○ loyal ○ untrue ○ we'll ○ paer ○ you've
15. ○ sharing ○ unload ○ politely ○ to ○ foyal
16. ○ he's ○ toyes ○ lately ○ crown ○ racing
17. ○ din't ○ hour ○ serving ○ power ○ distrust
18. ○ greate ○ recopy ○ I'd ○ pear ○ about
19. ○ I've ○ hoping ○ nicely ○ untuched ○ shouldn't
20. ○ disobey ○ kroud ○ unchanged ○ closely ○ regroup

Writing and Proofreading Guide

1. Choose a topic to write about.

2. Write your ideas. Don't worry about mistakes.

3. Now organize your writing so that it makes sense.

4. Proofread your work.
   Use these proofreading marks to make changes.

   ## Proofreading Marks

◯	spelling mistake
≡	capital letter
⊙	add period
⌃	add something
⌄	add apostrophe
ℓ	take out something
¶	indent paragraph
/	make small letter

   did you see the ~~the~~ spider ◯makeng◯ a web?

5. Write your final copy.
   Did you see the spider making a web?

6. Share your writing.

Using Your Dictionary

The *Spelling Workout* Dictionary shows you many things about your spelling words.

The **entry word** listed in alphabetical order is the word you are looking up.

The **sound-spelling** or **respelling** tells how to pronounce the word.

The **part of speech** is given as an abbreviation.

im·prove (im prōōv′) *v.* **1** to make or become better [Business has *improved*.] **2** to make good use of [She *improved* her spare time by reading.] —**im·proved′**, **im·prov′ing**

Sample sentences or **phrases** show how to use the word.

Other **forms** of the word are given.

The **definition** tells what the word means. There may be more than one definition.

Pronunciation Key

SYMBOL	KEY WORDS	SYMBOL	KEY WORDS	SYMBOL	KEY WORDS	SYMBOL	KEY WORDS
a	ask, fat	͞o	look, pull	b	bed, dub	t	top, hat
ā	ape, date	y͞o	unite, cure	d	did, had	v	vat, have
ä	car, lot	o͞o	ooze, tool	f	fall, off	w	will, always
		yo͞o	cute, few	g	get, dog	y	yet, yard
e	elf, ten	ou	out, crowd	h	he, ahead	z	zebra, haze
er	berry, care			j	joy, jump		
ē	even, meet	u	up, cut	k	kill, bake	ch	chin, arch
		ʉ	fur, fern	l	let, ball	ŋ	ring, singer
i	is, hit			m	met, trim	sh	she, dash
ir	mirror, here	ə	a in ago	n	not, ton	th	thin, truth
ī	ice, fire		e in agent	p	put, tap	*th*	then, father
			e in father	r	red, dear	zh	s in pleasure
ō	open, go		i in unity	s	sell, pass		
ô	law, horn		o in collect				
oi	oil, point		u in focus				

An Americanism is a word or usage of a word that was born in this country. An open star (☆) before an entry word or definition means that the word or definition is an Americanism.

Aa

a·bout (ə bout´) **adv. 1** on every side; all around [look *about*] **2** nearly; more or less [*about* ten years old] ◆**adj.** active; awake or recovered [At dawn I was up and *about*.] ◆**prep. 1** almost ready [I am *about* to cry.] **2** having to do with [a book *about* ships]

a·cross (ə krôs´) **adv.** from one side to the other [The new bridge makes it easy to get *across* in a car.] ◆**prep. 1** from one side to the other [We swam *across* the river.] **2** on the other side of [They live *across* the street.]

act (akt) **n. 1** a thing done; deed [an *act* of bravery] **2** one of the main divisions of a play, opera, etc. [The first *act* takes place in a palace.] ◆**v. 1** to play the part of, as on a stage [She *acted* Juliet.] **2** to behave like [Don't *act* the fool.]

ad·mit (əd mit´) **v. 1** to permit or give the right to enter [One ticket *admits* two people.] **2** to take or accept as being true; confess [Lucy will not *admit* her mistake.] —**ad·mit´ted, ad·mit´ting**

ad·ver·tise (ad´vər tīz´) **v. 1** to tell about a product in public and in such a way as to make people want to buy it [to *advertise* cars on television] **2** to announce or ask for publicly, as in a newspaper [to *advertise* a house for rent; to *advertise* for a cook] —**ad´ver·tis´ed, ad´ver·tis´ing** —**ad´ver·tis´er n.**

af·ford (ə fôrd´) **v.** to have money enough to spare for [Can we *afford* a new car?]

af·ter·noon (af´tər noon´) **n.** the time of day from noon to evening

a·gain (ə gen´) **adv.** once more; a second time [If you don't understand the sentence, read it *again*.]

age (āj) **n. 1** the time that a person or thing has existed from birth or beginning [He started school at the *age* of four.] **2** the fact of being old [Gray hair comes with *age*.]

air·plane (er´plān) **n.** an aircraft that is kept up by the force of air upon its wings and driven forward by a jet engine or propeller

air·port (er´pôrt) **n.** a place where aircraft can take off and land, get fuel, or take on passengers

a·live (ə līv´) **adj. 1** having life; living **2** going on; in action; not ended or destroyed [to keep old memories *alive*] **3** lively; alert

☆**al·ler·gy** (al´ər jē´) **n.** a condition in which one becomes sick, gets a rash, etc., by breathing in, touching, eating, or drinking something that is not harmful to most people [Hay fever is usually caused by an *allergy* to certain pollens.] —*pl.* **al´ler·gies**

al·low (ə lou´) **v. 1** to let be done; permit; let [*Allow* us to pay. No smoking *allowed*.] **2** to give or keep an extra amount so as to have enough [*Allow* an inch for shrinkage.]

all right (ôl rīt´) **adj. 1** good enough; satisfactory; adequate [Your work is *all right*.] ◆**adv. 2** yes; very well [*All right*, I'll do it.]

al·most (ôl´mōst) **adv.** not completely but very nearly [He tripped and *almost* fell. Sue is *almost* ten.]

al·read·y (ôl red´ē) **adv. 1** by or before this time [When we arrived, dinner had *already* begun.] **2** even now [I am *already* ten minutes late.]

al·though (ôl thō´) **conj.** in spite of the fact that; even if; though [*Although* the book was very long, he enjoyed it.]

al·to·geth·er (ôl´too geth´ ər) **adv.** to the full extent; wholly; completely [You're not *altogether* wrong.]

al·ways (ôl´wāz) **adv.** at all times; at every time [*Always* be courteous.]

an·chor (aŋ´kər) **n.** a heavy object let down into the water by a chain or rope to keep a ship or boat from drifting ◆**v.** to keep from drifting by using an *anchor* [to *anchor* the boat and go ashore]

an·gry (aŋ´grē) **adj. 1** feeling or showing anger [*angry* words; an *angry* crowd] **2** wild and stormy [an *angry* sea] —**an´gri·er, an´gri·est**

airplane

a	ask, fat
ā	ape, date
ä	car, lot
e	elf, ten
ē	even, meet
i	is, hit
ī	ice, fire
ō	open, go
ô	law, horn
oi	oil, point
oo	look, pull
oo	ooze, tool
ou	out, crowd
u	up, cut
ʉ	fur, fern
ə	**a** in ago
	e in agent
	e in father
	i in unity
	o in collect
	u in focus
ch	**ch**in, ar**ch**
ŋ	ri**ng**, si**ng**er
sh	**sh**e, da**sh**
th	**th**in, tru**th**
th	**th**en, fa**th**er
zh	s in plea**s**ure

151

an·y (en'ē) *adj.* **1** one, no matter which one, of more than two [*Any* pupil may answer.] **2** some, no matter how much, how many, or what kind [Do you have *any* apples?] ◆*pron.* any one or ones; any amount or number [I lost my pencils; do you have *any*?]

an·y·how (en'ē hou') *adv.* **1** no matter what else may be true; in any case [I don't like the color, and, *anyhow,* it's not my size.] **2** no matter in what way [That's a fine report *anyhow* you look at it.]

an·y·one (en'ē wun') *pron.* any person; anybody [Does *anyone* know where the house is?]

an·y·way (en'ē wā') *adv.* nevertheless; anyhow

ap·pear (ə pir') *v.* to come into sight or into being [A ship *appeared* on the horizon. Leaves *appear* on the tree every spring.]

ar·my (är'mē) *n.* **1** a large group of soldiers trained for war, especially on land; all the soldiers of a country **2** any large group of persons or animals [An *army* of workers was building the bridge.] —*pl.* **ar'mies**

Au·gust (ô'gəst) *n.* the eighth month of the year, which has 31 days; abbreviated **Aug.**

a·void (ə void') *v.* to keep away from; get out of the way of; shun [to *avoid* crowds]

a·wake (ə wāk') *v.* to come out of sleep; wake —**a·woke'** or **a·waked', a·waked'** or **a·wok'en, a·wak'ing** ◆*adj.* not asleep [I was *awake* all night.]

aw·ful (ô'fəl) *adj.* **1** making one feel awe or dread; causing fear [an *awful* scene of destruction] **2** very bad, ugly, great, etc.: *used only in everyday talk* [an *awful* joke; an *awful* fool]

awk·ward (ôk'wərd *or* äk'wərd) *adj.* not having grace or skill; clumsy; bungling [an *awkward* dancer]

aye or **ay** (ī) *adv.* yes ◆*n.* a vote of "yes"

ba·by (bā'bē) *n.* **1** a very young child; infant **2** a person who seems helpless, cries easily, etc. [like a *baby*] **3** the youngest or smallest in a group —*pl.* **ba'bies**

bake (bāk) *v.* to cook in an oven, with little or no liquid [I *baked* a cake.] —**baked, bak'ing**

bam·boo (bam boo') *n.* a tropical plant with woody stems that are hollow and jointed

ba·sic (bā'sik) *adj.* serving as a basis; main [These are the *basic* rules of the game.]

beach (bēch) *n.* a stretch of sand and pebbles at the edge of a sea, lake, or other body of water —*pl.* **beach'es**

be·cause (bē kôz') *conj.* for the reason that; since [I'm late *because* I overslept.]

be·fore (bē fôr') *prep.* earlier than; previous to [Will you finish *before* noon?] ◆*adv.* in the past; earlier [I've heard that song *before*.] ◆*conj.* earlier than the time that [Think *before* you speak.]

be·gin·ning (bē gin'iŋ) *n.* a start or starting; first part or first action [We came in just after the *beginning* of the movie. Going to the dance together was the *beginning* of our friendship.]

be·half (bē haf') *n.* support for someone; interest [Many of his friends spoke in his *behalf*.]

be·long (bē lôŋ') *v.* **1** to have its proper place [This chair *belongs* in the corner.] **2** to be owned by someone [This book *belongs* to you.]

be·low (bē lō') *adv., adj.* in or to a lower place; beneath [I'll take the upper bunk and you can sleep *below*.] ◆*prep.* lower than in place, position, price, rank, etc. [the people living *below* us; a price *below* $25]

bench (bench) *n.* a long, hard seat for several persons, with or without a back

be·neath (bē nēth′) **adv.** in a lower place; below or just below; underneath [Look *beneath* the table.] ◆**prep.** lower than; below or just below; under [the ground *beneath* my feet]

ber·ry (ber′ē) **n.** any small, juicy fruit with seeds and a soft pulp, as a strawberry, blackberry, or blueberry —*pl.* **ber′ries**

be·side (bē sīd′) **prep.** by or at the side of; close to [The garage is *beside* the house.]

best (best) **adj.** above all others in worth or ability; most excellent, most fit, most desirable, etc. [Joan is the *best* player on the team. When is the *best* time to plant tulips?] ◆**adv.** **1** in a way that is best or most excellent, fit, etc. [Which choir sang *best*?] **2** more than any other; most [Of all your books, I like that one *best*.] ◆**n.** **1** a person or thing that is most excellent, most fit, etc. [That doctor is among the *best* in the profession. When I buy shoes, I buy the *best*.] **2** the most that can be done; utmost [We did our *best* to win.]

bet·ter (bet′ər) **adj.** **1** above another, as in worth or ability; more excellent, more fit, more desirable, etc. [Grace is a *better* player than Chris. I have a *better* idea.] **2** not so sick; more healthy than before ◆**adv.** **1** in a way that is better or more excellent, fit, etc. [They will sing *better* with more practice.] **2** more [I like the orange drink *better* than the lime.]

big (big) **adj.** of great size; large [a *big* cake; a *big* city] —**big′ger, big′gest** —**big′ness n.**

bind (bīnd) **v.** to tie tightly together with rope or something similar [*Bind* logs together to make a raft.] —**bound, bind′ing**

bird (bʉrd) **n.** a warmblooded animal that has a backbone, two feet, two wings, and is covered with feathers; they lay eggs and can usually fly

bi·son (bī′sən) **n.** a wild animal that is related to the ox, with a shaggy mane, short, curved horns, and a humped back: the American bison is often called a **buffalo** —*pl.* **bi′son**

blame (blām) **v.** to say or think that someone or something is the cause of what is wrong or bad [Don't *blame* others for your own mistakes.] —**blamed, blam′ing** ◆**n.** the fact of being the cause of what is wrong or bad [I will take the *blame* for the broken window.]

blast (blast) **n.** a strong rush of air or gust of wind ◆**v.** to blow up with an explosive [to *blast* rock]

blaze (blāz) **n.** a bright flame or fire ◆**v.** to burn brightly —**blazed, blaz′ing**

blew (blo͞o) *past tense of* **blow**

blind (blīnd) **adj.** not able to see; having no sight ◆**v.** to make blind; make unable to see ◆**n.** a window shade of stiffened cloth, metal slats, etc.

blood (blud) **n.** the red liquid that is pumped through the arteries and veins by the heart; carries oxygen and cell-building material to the body tissues and carries carbon dioxide and waste material away from them

blouse (blous) **n.** a loose outer garment like a shirt, worn by women and children

blow (blō) **v.** **1** to move with some force [There is a wind *blowing*.] **2** to force air out from the mouth [*Blow* on your hands to warm them.] —**blew, blow′ing** ◆**n.** **1** the act of blowing **2** a strong wind; gale

blue (blo͞o) **adj.** having the color of the clear sky or the deep sea —**blu′er, blu′est**

bod·y (bäd′ē) **n.** the whole physical part of a person or animal [Athletes have strong *bodies*.]

bot·tom (bät′əm) **n.** the lowest part [Sign your name at the *bottom* of this paper.] ◆**adj.** of or at the lowest part [the *bottom* shelf].

bought (bôt) *past tense and past participle of* **buy**

bou·quet (bo͞o kā′ *or* bō kā′) **n.** a bunch of cut flowers [a *bouquet* of roses]

box (bäks) **n.** a four-sided container with a bottom and a lid used for holding or carrying things —*pl.* **box′es**

brag (brag) **v.** to talk about with too much pride and pleasure —**bragged, brag′ging**

a	ask, fat
ā	ape, date
ä	car, lot
e	elf, ten
ē	even, meet
i	is, hit
ī	ice, fire
ō	open, go
ô	law, horn
οi	oil, point
σσ	look, pull
o͞o	ooze, tool
ου	out, crowd
u	up, cut
ʉ	fur, fern
ə	a in ago
	e in agent
	e in father
	i in unity
	o in collect
	u in focus
ch	chin, arch
ŋ	ring, singer
sh	she, dash
th	thin, truth
th	then, father
zh	s in pleasure

153

cage

branch (branch) *n.* any part of a tree growing from the trunk or from a main limb —*pl.* **branch´es** ◆*v.* to divide into branches [The road *branches* two miles east of town.]

brave (brāv) *adj.* willing to face danger; not afraid [We had a *brave* leader on our canoeing trip.] —**brav´er, brav´est**

break (brāk) *v.* **1** to come or make come apart by force; split or crack sharply into pieces [*Break* an egg into the bowl. The rusty hinge *broke*.] **2** to do better than; outdo [He *broke* the record for running the mile.] —**broke, bro´ken, break´ing** ◆*n.* **1** a broken place [The X-ray showed a *break* in the bone.] **2** an interruption [Recess is a relaxing *break* in our school day.]

breathe (brēth) *v.* to take air into the lungs and then let it out [to *breathe* deeply] —**breathed, breath´ing**

bright (brīt) *adj.* **1** shining; giving light; full of light [a *bright* star; a *bright* day] **2** having a quick mind; clever [a *bright* child] —**bright´ly** *adv.* —**bright´ness** *n.*

bring (briŋ) *v.* to carry or lead here or to the place where the speaker will be [*Bring* it to my house tomorrow.] —**brought, bring´ing**

bro·ken (brō´kən) *past participle of* **break** ◆*adj.* **1** split or cracked into pieces [a *broken* dish; a *broken* leg] **2** not in working condition [a *broken* watch]

brook (brook) *n.* a small stream

broom (broom) *n.* a brush with a long handle, used for sweeping

brought (brôt *or* brät) *past tense and past participle of* **bring**

brush (brush) *n.* a bunch of bristles, hairs, or wires fastened into a hard back or handle used for cleaning, polishing, grooming, painting, etc. —*pl.* **brush´es** ◆*v.* **1** to use a brush on; clean, polish, paint, smooth, etc. with a brush [*Brush* your shoes. *Brush* the paint on evenly.] **2** to touch or graze in passing [The tire of the car *brushed* against the curb.]

buf·fa·lo (buf´ə lō) *n.* **1** a wild ox of Africa and Asia that is sometimes used as a work animal **2** *another name for* the North American **bison** —*pl.* **buf´fa·loes** or **buf´fa·los** or **buf´fa·lo**

bunch (bunch) *n.* a group of things of the same kind growing or placed together [a *bunch* of bananas; a *bunch* of keys] —*pl.* **bunch´es**

bush (boosh) *n.* a woody plant, smaller than a tree and having many stems branching out low instead of one main stem or trunk; shrub —*pl.* **bush´es**

busi·ness (biz´nəs) *n.* **1** what a person does for a living; a person's work or occupation [Her *business* is writing plays.] **2** a place where things are made or sold; store or factory [Raul owns three *businesses*.] —*pl.* **bus´i·ness·es**

butterfly (but´ər flī) *n.* an insect with a slender body and four broad, usually brightly colored wings —*pl.* **but´ter·flies**

buy (bī) *v.* to get by paying money or something else [The Dutch *bought* Manhattan Island for about $24.] —**bought, buy´ing** ◆*n.* the value of a thing compared with its price [Turnips are your best *buy* in January vegetables.]

Cc

cage (kāj) *n.* a box or closed-off space with wires or bars on the sides, in which to keep birds or animals ◆*v.* to shut up in a cage —**caged, cag´ing**

calf¹ (kaf) *n.* **1** a young cow or bull **2** a young elephant, whale, hippopotamus, seal, etc. —*pl.* **calves**

calf² (kaf) *n.* the fleshy back part of the leg between the knee and the ankle —*pl.* **calves**

camp (kamp) *n.* a place in the country where people, especially children, can have an outdoor vacation ◆*v.* to live in a camp or in the outdoors for a time [We'll be *camping* in Michigan this summer.]

can·dy (kan′dē) *n.* a sweet food made from sugar or syrup, with flavor, coloring, fruits, nuts, etc., added —*pl.* **can′dies**

can·not (kan′ät *or* kə nät′) *the usual way of writing* **can not**

can·vas (kan′vəs) *n.* **1** a strong, heavy cloth of hemp, cotton, or linen, used for tents, sails, or oil paintings —*pl.* **can′vas·es**

care (ker) *n.* a watching over or tending; protection [The books were left in my *care*.] ◆*v.* **1** to watch over or take charge of something [Will you *care* for my canary while I'm gone?] **2** to feel a liking [I don't *care* for dancing.] —**cared, car′ing**

car·go (kär′gō) *n.* the load of goods carried by a ship, airplane, or truck —*pl.* **car′goes** or **car′gos**

car·pet (kär′pət) *n.* a thick, heavy fabric used to cover floors ◆*v.* to cover with a carpet or with something like a carpet [The lawn was *carpeted* with snow.]

car·ry (kar′ē) *v.* to take from one place to another; transport or conduct [Please help me *carry* these books home. The large pipe *carries* water. Air *carries* sounds.] —**car′ried, car′ry·ing**

case (kās) *n.* a container for holding and protecting something [a violin *case*]

catch (kach) *v.* **1** to stop by grasping with the hands or arms [to *catch* a ball] **2** to become sick or infected with [to *catch* the flu] —**caught, catch′ing** ◆*n.* **1** the act of catching a ball, etc. [The outfielder made a running *catch*.] **2** anything that is caught [a *catch* of 14 fish]

cat·tle (kat′l) *pl. n.* animals of the cow family that are raised on farms and ranches, as cows, bulls, steers, and oxen

caught (kôt) *past tense and past participle of* **catch**

cent (sent) *n.* a coin worth one hundredth part of a dollar; penny

chair (cher) *n.* a piece of furniture that has a back and is a seat for one person

chalk (chôk) *n.* **1** a whitish limestone that is soft and easily crushed into a powder, made up mainly of tiny sea shells **2** a piece of chalk or material like it, for writing on chalkboards

cham·pi·on (cham′pē ən′) *n.* a person, animal, or thing that wins first place or is judged to be best in a contest or sport [a spelling *champion*]

chap·ter (chap′tər) *n.* any of the main parts into which a book is divided

chart (chärt) *n.* **1** a map, especially one for use in steering a ship or guiding an aircraft [A sailor's *chart* shows coastlines, depths, currents, etc.] **2** a group of facts about something set up in the form of a diagram, graph, table, etc. ◆*v.* to make a map of

cheap (chēp) *adj.* low in price [Vegetables are *cheaper* in summer than in winter.] ◆*adv.* at a low cost [I bought these shoes *cheap* at a sale.] —**cheap′ly** *adv.* —**cheap′ness** *n.*

check (chek) *n.* **1** the mark √, used to show that something is right or to call attention to something **2** a written order to a bank to pay a certain amount of money from one's account to a certain person ☆◆*v.* to prove to be right or find what is wanted by examining, comparing, etc. [These figures *check* with mine. *Check* the records for this information.]

cheer (chir) *n.* **1** a glad, excited shout of welcome, joy, or approval [The crowd gave the team three *cheers*.] **2** good or glad feelings; joy, hope, etc. [a visit that brought *cheer* to the invalid] ◆*v.* **1** to make or become glad or hopeful [Things are getting better, so *cheer* up!] **2** to urge on or applaud with cheers

chew·y (chōō′ē) *adj.* needing much chewing [*chewy* candy] —**chew′i·er, chew′i·est**

chair

a	ask, fat
ā	ape, date
ä	car, lot
e	elf, ten
ē	even, meet
i	is, hit
ī	ice, fire
ō	open, go
ô	law, horn
oi	oil, point
ᴏᴏ	look, pull
ᴏ̄ᴏ̄	ooze, tool
ou	out, crowd
u	up, cut
ʉ	fur, fern
ə	a in ago
	e in agent
	e in father
	i in unity
	o in collect
	u in focus
ch	chin, arch
ŋ	ring, singer
sh	she, dash
th	thin, truth
th	then, father
zh	s in pleasure

child (chīld) **n. 1** a baby; infant **2** a young boy or girl **3** a son or daughter [Their *children* are all grown up.] —*pl.* **chil´dren**

chil·dren (chil´drən) **n.** *plural of* **child**

chim·ney (chim´nē) **n.** a pipe or shaft going up through a roof to carry off smoke from a furnace, fireplace, or stove: usually enclosed with brick or stone —*pl.* **chim´neys**

choice (chois) **n. 1** the act of choosing or picking; selection [You may have a dessert of your own *choice*.] **2** a person or thing chosen [Green is my *choice* for mayor.] —**choic´er, choic´est**

choose (cho͞oz) **v.** to pick out one or more from a number or group [*Choose* a subject from this list.] —**chose, cho´sen, choos´ing**

chop (chäp) **v. 1** to cut by strokes with a sharp tool [to *chop* down a tree] —**chopped, chop´ping**

churn (churn) **n.** a container in which milk or cream is stirred hard or shaken to make butter ◆**v.** to use a churn to make butter [to *churn* milk or cream]

claim (klām) **v.** to ask for something that one thinks one has a right to [He *claimed* the package at the post office.] **n. 1** a demand for something that one thinks one has a right to **2** something said as a fact that may or may not be true

clap (klap) **v.** to make a sudden, loud sound like that of two flat surfaces being struck together [I *clapped* my hands.] —**clapped, clap´ping**

class (klas) **n.** ☆a group of students meeting together to be taught; also, a meeting of this kind [My English *class* is held at 9 o'clock.] —*pl.* **class´es**

clean (klēn) **adj. 1** without dirt or impure matter [*clean* dishes; *clean* oil] **2** neat and tidy [to keep a *clean* desk] ◆**v.** to make clean [Please *clean* the oven.]

clear (klir) **adj. 1** bright or sunny; without clouds or mist [a *clear* day] **2** that can be seen through; transparent [*clear* glass] **3** without anything in the way; not blocked; open [a *clear* view; a *clear* passage] ◆**adv.** in a clear manner; clearly [The bells rang out *clear*.] —**clear´ly** ◆**v.** to empty or remove [*Clear* the snow from the sidewalk. Help me *clear* the table of dishes.] —**clear´ness n.**

climb (klīm) **v.** to go up, or sometimes down, by using the feet and often the hands [to *climb* the stairs; to *climb* up or down a tree] ◆**n.** the act of climbing; rise; ascent [a tiring *climb*] —**climb´er**

close (klōs) **adj. 1** with not much space between; near [The old houses are too *close* to each other.] **2** thorough or careful [Pay *close* attention.] —**clos´er, clos´est** ◆**adv.** so as to be close or near; closely [Follow *close* behind the leader.] —**close´ly adv.** —**close´ness n.**

clown (kloun) **n. 1** a person who entertains, as in a circus, by doing comical tricks and silly stunts; jester; buffoon **2** a person who likes to make jokes or act in a comical way [the *clown* of our family]

clue (klo͞o) **n.** a fact or thing that helps to solve a puzzle or mystery [Muddy footprints were a *clue* to the man's guilt.]

coach (kōch) **n. 1** a large, closed carriage drawn by horses, with the driver's seat outside **2** a person who teaches and trains students, athletes, singers, and so on ◆**v.** to teach, train, or tutor [Will you *coach* me for the test in history?]

coin (koin) **n.** a piece of metal money having a certain value

col·lar (käl´ər) **n. 1** the part of a garment that fits around the neck: sometimes a separate piece or a band that is folded over **2** the part of a horse's harness that fits around its neck

coin

com·ma (käm′ə) *n.* a punctuation mark (,) used to show a pause that is shorter than the pause at the end of a sentence: often used between clauses or after the opening phrase of a sentence; separates words, numbers, or phrases in a series

com·pare (kəm per′) *v.* **1** to describe as being the same; liken [The sound of thunder can be *compared* to the roll of drums.] **2** to examine certain things in order to find out how they are alike or different [How do the two cars *compare* in size and price?] —**com·pared′, com·par′ing**

cone (kōn) *n.* **1** a solid object that narrows evenly from a flat circle at one end to a point at the other **2** anything shaped like this, as a shell of pastry for holding ice cream **3** the fruit of some evergreen trees, containing the seeds

con·tain (kən tān′) *v.* to have in it; hold; enclose or include [This bottle *contains* cream. Your list *contains* 25 names.]

cook·ie (kook′ē) *n.* ☆a small, flat, sweet cake —*pl.* **cook′ies**

cool·er (kool′ər) *n.* a container or room in which things are cooled or kept cool

cop·y (käp′ē) *n.* **1** a thing made just like another; imitation or likeness [four carbon *copies* of a letter] **2** any one of a number of books, magazines, pictures, etc., with the same printed matter [a library with six *copies* of *Tom Sawyer*] —*pl.* **cop′ies** ◆*v.* **1** to make a copy or copies of [*Copy* the questions that are on the chalkboard.] **2** to act or be the same as; imitate —**cop′ied, cop′y·ing**

cost (kôst) *v.* to be priced at; be sold for [It *costs* a dime.] —**cost, cost′ing** ◆*n.* amount of money, time, work, etc., asked or paid for something; price [the high *cost* of meat]

cough (kôf) *v.* **1** to force air from the lungs with a sudden, loud noise, as to clear the throat **2** to get out of the throat by coughing [to *cough* up phlegm] ◆*n.* a condition of coughing often [I have a bad *cough*.]

could·n't (kood′nt) *contraction* could not

coun·try (kun′trē) *n.* **1** an area of land; region [wooded *country*] **2** the whole land of a nation [The *country* of Japan is made up of islands.] **3** land with farms and small towns; land outside of cities [Let's drive out to the *country*.] —*pl.* **coun′tries**

course (kôrs) *n.* **1** forward movement from one point to the next [We travel to New York several times in the *course* of a year.] **2** an area of land or water used for certain sports or games [a golf *course*]

court (kôrt) *n.* **1** an open space that is surrounded by buildings or walls **2** a space that is marked out for playing certain games [a basketball *court*] **3** a place where law trials are held

crack (krak) *v.* to break or split, with or without the parts falling apart [The snowball *cracked* the window.] ◆*n.* a break, usually with the parts still holding together [a *crack* in a cup]

crawl (krôl) *v.* to move slowly by dragging the body along the ground as a worm does ◆*n.* a crawling; slow, creeping movement

creek (krēk *or* krik) *n.* a small stream, a little larger than a brook

crick·et (krik′it) *n.* a leaping insect related to the grasshopper

cried (krīd) *past tense and past participle of* **cry**

crook·ed (krook′əd) *adj.* **1** not straight; bent, curved, or twisted [a *crooked* road] **2** not honest; cheating

crowd (kroud) *n.* a large group of people together [*crowds* of Christmas shoppers] ◆*v.* to push or squeeze [Can we all *crowd* into one car?]

crown (kroun) *n.* a headdress of gold, jewels, etc., worn by a king or queen ◆*v.* to make a king or queen by putting a crown on [Elizabeth I was *crowned* in 1558.]

cone

a	ask, fat
ā	ape, date
ä	car, lot
e	elf, ten
ē	even, meet
i	is, hit
ī	ice, fire
ō	open, go
ô	law, horn
oi	oil, point
oo	look, pull
oo	ooze, tool
ou	out, crowd
u	up, cut
ʉ	fur, fern
ə	a in ago
	e in agent
	e in father
	i in unity
	o in collect
	u in focus
ch	chin, arch
ŋ	ring, singer
sh	she, dash
th	thin, truth
th	then, father
zh	s in pleasure

deer

cry (krī) *v.* **1** to show sorrow or pain by shedding tears **2** to say loudly; to shout ["Help! Help!" the victim *cried*.] —**cries, cried, cry´ing** ◆*n.* a loud sound made by the voice

cube (ky$\overline{oo}$b) *n.* a solid object with six square sides that are the same size

cur·ly (kur´lē) *adj.* tending to curl [She has long, *curly* hair.] —**curl´i·er, curl´i·est**

cut (kut) *v.* **1** to make an opening in with a knife or other sharp tool; pierce; gash [Andy *cut* his chin while shaving.] **2** to divide into parts with such a tool; sever [Will you *cut* the cake?] **3** to make shorter by trimming [to *cut* one's hair] **4** to go through or across, usually to make a shorter way [The path *cuts* across the meadow. The tunnel *cuts* through the mountain.] —**cut, cut´ting**

Dd

dai·ly (dā´lē) *adj.* done every day or every weekday [*daily* exercises] ◆*adv.* every day [Feed the cat *daily*.]

Dal·las (dal´əs) a city in northeastern Texas

Dal·ma·tian (dal mā´shən) *n.* a large dog with short hair and a black-and-white coat

dance (dans) *v.* to move the body and feet in some kind of rhythm, usually to music [to *dance* a waltz or a minuet] —**danced, danc´ing**

dan·ger (dān´jər) *n.* **1** a condition in which there could be harm, trouble, loss, etc.; risk; peril [to live in constant *danger*]

dark (därk) *adj.* having little or no light [a *dark* night] —**dark´ness** *n.*

dash (dash) *v.* to move quickly; rush [The thief *dashed* down the alley.] ◆*n.* **1** a little bit; pinch [Put a *dash* of salt in the salad.] ☆**2** a short, fast run or race [a 100-yard *dash*] **3** the punctuation mark (—), used in printing or writing

dead (ded) *adj.* no longer living; without life [Throw out those *dead* flowers.] ◆*adv.* completely; entirely [I am *dead* tired from running.] ◆*n.* the time of most cold, most darkness, etc. [the *dead* of winter; the *dead* of night] —**dead´ly** *adv.*

deer (dir) *n.* a swift-running, hoofed animal that chews its cud: the male usually has antlers that are shed every year —*pl.* **deer**

de·pend (dē pend´) *v.* **1** to be controlled or decided by [The attendance at the game *depends* on the weather.] **2** to put one's trust in; be sure of [You can't *depend* on this weather.] **3** to rely on for help or support [They *depend* on their parents for money.]

desk (desk) *n.* a piece of furniture with a smooth top at which one can write, draw, or read: often has drawers for storing things

des·sert (də zurt´) *n.* something sweet served at the end of a meal

de·stroy (dē stroi´) *v.* to put an end to by breaking up, tearing down, ruining, or spoiling [The flood *destroyed* 300 homes.]

de·vice (dē vīs´) *n.* something made or invented for some special use [A windmill is a *device* for putting wind power to work.]

di·al (dī´əl) *n.* **1** the face of an instrument such as a clock **2** a disk that can be turned or a set of push buttons on a telephone, television, radio, or gauge ◆*v.* **1** to tune in a radio or television station **2** to call on a telephone by using a dial [I *dialed* his number.]

dia·mond (dī´mənd *or* dī´ə mənd) *n.* a very precious stone, often colorless

did·n't (did´nt) *contraction* did not

die (dī) *v.* to stop living; become dead —**died, dy´ing**

di·et (dī´ət) *n.* what a person or animal usually eats or drinks ◆*v.* to eat certain kinds and amounts of food, especially in order to lose weight

dig (dig) **v.** **1** to turn up or remove ground with a spade, the hands, claws, etc. [The children are *digging* in the sand.] **2** to make by digging [to *dig* a well] —**dug** or *in older use* **digged, dig´ging**

dim (dim) **adj.** not bright or clear; somewhat dark; shadowy; gloomy [the *dim* twilight] —**dim´mer, dim´mest**

dis·ap·pear (dis′ə pir′) **v.** to stop being seen or to stop existing; vanish [The car *disappeared* around a curve. Dinosaurs *disappeared* millions of years ago.] —**dis′ap·pear´ance n.**

dis·cov·er (dis kuv′ər) **v.** to be the first to find, see, or learn about [Marie and Pierre Curie *discovered* radium.]

dish (dish) **n.** any of the plates, bowls, saucers, etc., used to serve food at the table —*pl.* **dish´es** ➤**v.** to serve in a dish [*Dish* up the beans.] —**dish´ful adj.**

dis·like (dis līk′) **v.** to have a feeling of not liking; be opposed to [I *dislike* people I can't trust.] —**dis·liked´, dis·lik´ing** ➤**n.** a feeling of not liking; distaste [The gardener felt a strong *dislike* for toads.]

dis·o·bey (dis′ō bā′) **v.** to fail to obey or refuse to obey

dis·or·der (dis ôr′dər) **n.** lack of order; jumble; confusion [The troops retreated in *disorder*.]

dis·please (dis plēz′) **v.** to make angry or not satisfied; annoy —**dis′·pleased´, dis′·pleas´ing**

dis·re·spect (dis′rē spekt′) **n.** lack of respect or politeness; rudeness —**dis′re·spect´ful adj.** —**dis′re·spect´ful·ly adv.**

dis·taste (dis tāst′) **n.** dislike; aversion [a *distaste* for worms]

dis·trust (dis trust′) **n.** a lack of trust; doubt; suspicion ➤**v.** to have no trust in; doubt —**dis·trust´ful adj.**

ditch (dich) **n.** a long, narrow opening dug in the earth, as for carrying off water; trench [a *ditch* along the road]

di·vide (də vīd′) **v.** **1** to separate into parts [A stream *divides* the valley.] **2** to find out how many times one number is contained in another [If you *divide* 12 by 3, you get 4.] —**di·vid´ed, di·vid´ing**

do (do͞o) **v.** **1** to work at or carry out an action; perform [What *do* you *do* for a living? I'll *do* the job.] **2** to bring about; cause [The storm *did* a lot of damage.] **3** to put forth; exert [She *did* her best.] **4** to take care of; attend to [Who will *do* the dishes?] —**did, done, do´ing**

does (duz) *the form of the verb* **do** *showing the present time with singular nouns and with* he, she, *or* it

does·n't (duz′nt) *contraction* does not

don't (dōnt) *contraction* do not

doubt (dout) **v.** **1** to think that something may not be true or right; be unsure of; question [I *doubt* that this is the correct answer.] **2** to consider unlikely [I *doubt* it will snow today.] ➤**n.** a feeling of not being sure or certain of [I have no *doubt* that you will return safely.]

dress·ing (dres′iŋ) **n.** **1** a bandage or medicine for a wound or sore **2** a sauce, as of oil, vinegar, and seasoning, added to salads and other dishes **3** a stuffing, as of bread and seasoning, for roast chicken, turkey, etc.

drive (drīv) **v.** to control the movement of an automobile, horse and wagon, bus, etc. —**drove, driv´en, driv´ing** ➤**n.** **1** a trip in an automobile, etc. **2** a street, road, or driveway

drove (drōv) *past tense of* **drive**

drown (droun) **v.** to die from being under water, where the lungs can get no air [to fall overboard and *drown*]

dry (drī) **adj.** **1** not wet or damp; without moisture **2** having little or no rain or water [a *dry* summer] **3** thirsty —**dri´er, dri´est** ➤**v.** to make or become dry —**dried, dry´ing** —**dry´ly adv.** —**dry´ness n.**

dug (dug) *past tense and past participle of* **dig**

a	ask, fat
ā	ape, date
ä	car, lot
e	elf, ten
ē	even, meet
i	is, hit
ī	ice, fire
ō	open, go
ô	law, horn
oi	oil, point
o͝o	look, pull
o͞o	ooze, tool
ou	out, crowd
u	up, cut
ʉ	fur, fern
ə	**a** in ago
	e in agent
	e in father
	i in unity
	o in collect
	u in focus
ch	chin, arch
ŋ	ring, singer
sh	she, dash
th	thin, truth
th	then, father
zh	s in pleasure

Ee

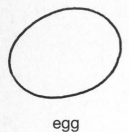

egg

each (ēch) *adj., pron.* every one of two or more, thought of separately [*Each* pupil will receive a book. *Each* of the books is numbered.] ◆*adv.* apiece [Tickets cost $5 *each.*]

ea·ger (ē′gər) *adj.* wanting very much; anxious to do or get [*eager* to win; *eager* for praise] —**ea′ger·ly** *adv.* —**ea′ger·ness** *n.*

ear·ly (ur′lē) *adv., adj.* **1** near the beginning; soon after the start [in the *early* afternoon; *early* in his career] **2** before the usual or expected time [The bus arrived *early.*] —**ear′li·er, ear′li·est** —**ear′li·ness** *n.*

earn (urn) *v.* **1** to get as pay for work done [She *earns* $10 an hour.] **2** to get or deserve because of something one has done [At the Olympics she *earned* a gold medal for swimming.]

earth (urth) *n.* **1** the planet that we live on; the fifth largest planet and the third in distance away from the sun **2** the dry part of the earth's surface that is not the sea **3** soil or ground [a flowerpot filled with good, rich *earth*]

eas·i·ly (ē′z′lē) *adv.* without trying too hard; with no trouble

east (ēst) *n.* **1** the direction toward the point where the sun rises **2** a place or region in or toward this direction ◆*adj.* in, of, to, or toward the east [the *east* bank of the river] ◆*adv.* in or toward the east [Go *east* ten miles.]

eas·y (ē′zē) *adj.* not hard to do, learn or get [an *easy* job] —**eas′i·er, eas′i·est**

egg (eg) *n.* the oval or round body that is laid by a female bird, fish, reptile, insect, etc., and from which a young bird, fish, etc., is later hatched: it has a brittle shell or tough outer skin

eight (āt) *n., adj.* one more than seven; the number 8

e·lect (i lekt′) *v.* to choose for an office by voting [We *elected* a new student council in September.]

el·e·phant (el′ə fənt) *n.* a huge animal with a thick skin, two ivory tusks, and a long snout, or trunk: it is found in Africa and India and is the largest of the four-legged animals

else (els) *adj.* **1** not the same; different; other [I thought you were someone *else.*] **2** that may be added; more [Do you want anything *else*?] ◆*adv.* in a different time, place, or way [Where *else* did you go?]

emp·ty (emp′tē) *adj.* having nothing or no one in it; not occupied; vacant [an *empty* jar; *empty* house] —**emp′ti·er, emp′ti·est** ◆*v.* to take out or pour out [*Empty* the dirty water in the sink.] —**emp′tied, emp′ty·ing** —*pl.* **emp′ties** —**emp′ti·ly** *adv.* —**emp′ti·ness** *n.*

en·joy (en joi′) *v.* to get joy or pleasure from [We *enjoyed* the baseball game.]

e·ven (ē′vən) *adj.* flat, level, or smooth [an *even* surface] ◆*adv.* though it may seem unlikely; indeed [*Even* a child could do it.] ◆*v.* to make or become level

ev·ery (ev′rē) *adj.* **1** all the group of which the thing named is one; each [*Every* student must take the test. She has read *every* book on the list.] **2** all that there could be [You've been given *every* chance.]

ev·er·y·bod·y (ev′rē bäd′ē *or* ev′rē bud′ē) *pron.* every person; everyone [*Everybody* loves a good story.]

ev·er·y·where (ev′rē hwer′) *adv.* in or to every place [*Everywhere* I go, I meet friends.]

ex·er·cise (ek′sər sīz′) *n.* the active use of the body in order to make it stronger or healthier [Long walks are good outdoor *exercise.*] ◆*v.* to put into use or do certain regular movements, in order to develop or train [I *exercise* every morning.]

ex·plain (ik splān′) **v.** to make clear or plain [The teacher *explained* the story to the class.]

eye (ī) **n.** the part of the body with which a human being or animal sees ◆**v.** to look at; observe [We *eyed* the stranger suspiciously.] **—eyed, ey′ing**

Ff

face (fās) **n.** the front part of the head, including the eyes, nose, and mouth ◆**v.** to turn toward or have the face turned toward [Please *face* the class. Our house *faces* a park.] **—faced, fac′ing**

fail (fāl) **v.** **1** to not do what one tried to do or what one should have done; not succeed; miss or neglect [She *failed* as a singer. He *failed* to keep his promise.] **2** to give or get a grade that shows one has not passed a test, a school course, etc.

fam·i·ly (fam′ə lē′) **n.** **1** a group made up of two parents and all of their children **2** a group of people who are related by marriage or a common ancestor; relatives; clan **—pl. fam′i·lies′**

farm·er (fär′mər) **n.** a person who owns or works on a farm

fast¹ (fast) **adj.** moving, working, etc., at high speed; rapid; quick; swift [a *fast* pace; a *fast* reader] ◆**adv.** **1** at a high speed; swiftly; rapidly [arrested for driving too *fast*] **2** in a complete way; soundly; thoroughly [*fast* asleep]

fast² (fast) **v.** to go without any food or certain foods, as in following the rules of one's religion

fax (faks) **n.** **1** an exact copy **2** pages sent and copied by electrical means, as by radio or wire **—pl. faxes** ◆**v.** to send by fax **—faxed, fax′ing**

fear (fir) **n.** the feeling one has when danger, pain, or trouble is near; feeling of being worried or excited or of wanting to run and hide [Jungle animals have a natural *fear* of lions.] ◆**v.** to feel fear of; be afraid of; dread [Even brave people can *fear* real danger.]

fear·less (fir′les) **adj.** having no fear; brave **—fear′less·ly adv.**

feast (fēst) **n.** a large meal with many courses; banquet ◆**v.** to eat a big or rich meal

feel (fēl) **v.** **1** to touch in order to find out something [*Feel* the baby's bottle to see if the milk is warm.] **2** to be aware of through the senses or the mind [He *felt* rain on his face. Do you *feel* pain in this tooth?] **3** to think or believe [She *feels* that we should go.] **—felt, feel′ing** ◆**n.** the way a thing feels to the touch [It seems to be all wool by the *feel* of it.]

felt¹ (felt) **n.** a heavy material made of wool, fur, or hair pressed together under heat ◆**adj.** made of felt [a *felt* hat]

felt² (felt) *past tense and past participle of* **feel**

fifth (fifth) **adj.** coming after four others; 5th in order ◆**n.** one of five equal parts of something; 1/5

fight (fīt) **v.** to use fists, weapons, or other force in trying to beat or overcome someone or something; battle; struggle [to *fight* hand to hand; to *fight* a war] **—fought, fight′ing** ◆**n.** the use of force to beat or overcome someone or something; battle

fin·ish (fin′ish) **v.** to bring or come to an end; complete or become completed [Did you *finish* your work? The game *finished* early.] ◆**n.** **1** the last part; end [The audience stayed to the *finish*.] **2** the kind of surface a thing has [an oil *finish* on wood] **—fin′ished adj.**

first (furst) **adj.** before another or before all others in time, order, quality, etc.; earliest, foremost, etc. [the *first* snow of winter; the *first* door to the right; *first* prize] ◆**adv.** before anything or anyone else [*First,* we had soup. Guests are served *first*.] ◆**n.** **1** the one that is first [to be the *first* to succeed] **2** the beginning; start [At *first*, I believed him.]

a	ask, fat
ā	ape, date
ä	car, lot
e	elf, ten
ē	even, meet
i	is, hit
ī	ice, fire
ō	open, go
ô	law, horn
oi	oil, point
oo	look, pull
ōō	ooze, tool
ou	out, crowd
u	up, cut
ʉ	fur, fern
ə	a in ago
	e in agent
	e in father
	i in unity
	o in collect
	u in focus
ch	chin, arch
ŋ	ring, singer
sh	she, dash
th	thin, truth
th	then, father
zh	s in pleasure

fish (fish) *n.* an animal that lives in water and has a backbone, fins, and gills for breathing: most fish are covered with scales —*pl.* **fish** (or when different kinds are meant, **fishes**) [She caught three *fish*. The aquarium exhibits many *fishes*.] ◆*v.* to catch or try to catch fish

five (fīv) *n., adj.* one more than four; the number 5

flaw (flô) *n.* a break, scratch, crack, etc., that spoils something; blemish [There is a *flaw* in this diamond.] —**flaw′less** *adj.* —**flaw′less·ly** *adv.*

flex (fleks) *v.* **1** to bend [to *flex* an arm] **2** to make tighter and harder; contract [to *flex* a muscle]

flight (flīt) *n.* **1** the act or way of flying or moving through space [the swift *flight* of birds] **2** a trip through the air [a long *flight* from Los Angeles to New York]

float (flōt) *v.* **1** to rest on top of water or other liquid and not sink [Ice *floats*.] **2** to move or drift slowly, as on a liquid or through the air [Clouds *floated* overhead.] ◆*n.* a platform on wheels that carries a display or exhibit in a parade —**float′er**

flood (flud) *n.* an overflowing of water onto a place that is usually dry ◆*v.* to flow over its banks onto nearby land [The river *floods* every spring.]

floor (flôr) *n.* the bottom part of a room, hall, etc., on which to walk

flow·er (flou′ər) *n.* the part of a plant that bears the seed and usually has brightly colored petals; blossom or bloom ◆*v.* to come into bloom; bear flowers

flute (flo͞ot) *n.* a woodwind instrument with a high pitch, shaped like a long, thin tube

fly[1] (flī) *v.* **1** to move through the air by using wings, as a bird **2** to travel or carry through the air, as in an aircraft —**flew, flown, fly′ing**

fly[2] (flī) *n.* a flying insect having one pair of wings, as the housefly and gnat —*pl.* **flies**

fish

fog (fôg *or* fäg) *n.* **1** a large mass of tiny drops of water, near the earth's surface; thick mist that makes it hard to see **2** a condition of being confused or bewildered —**fogged, fog′ging**

foil[1] (foil) *v.* to keep from doing something; thwart; stop [Their evil plans were *foiled* again.]

foil[2] (foil) *n.* a very thin sheet of metal [aluminum *foil*]

for·est (fôr′əst) *n.* many trees growing closely together over a large piece of land; large woods ◆*v.* to plant with trees

fork (fôrk) *n.* **1** a tool with a handle at one end and two or more points or prongs at the other, used to pick up something: small forks are used in eating, and large forks, as pitchforks, are used for tossing hay and manure on a farm ☆**2** the point where something divides into two or more branches [the *fork* of a road or of a tree] ◆*v.* to divide into branches [Go left where the road *forks*.]

for·ward (fôr′wərd) *adj.* at, toward, or of the front [the *forward* part] ◆*adv.* to the front; ahead [We moved slowly *forward* in the ticket line.]

fought (fôt) *past tense and past participle of* **fight**

fourth (fôrth) *adj.* coming after three others; 4th in order ◆*n.* one of four equal parts of something; 1/4

free (frē) *adj.* **1** not under the control of another; not a slave or not in prison **2** able to vote and to speak, write, meet, and worship as one pleases; having political and civil liberty **3** not tied up, fastened, or shut in; loose [As soon as the bird was *free*, it flew away.] **4** with no charge; without cost [*free* tickets to the ball game] —**fre′er, fre′est** ◆*v.* to make free [The governor *freed* five prisoners by granting pardons.] —**freed, free′ing**

freeze (frēz) *v.* to harden into ice; make or become solid because of cold [Water *freezes* at 0°C or 32°F.] —**froze, freez′ing**

freight (frāt) *n.* a load of goods shipped by train, truck, ship, or airplane

fresh (fresh) *adj.* **1** newly made, got, or grown; not spoiled, stale, etc. [*fresh* coffee; *fresh* eggs] **2** cool and clean [*fresh* air] —**fresh´ly** *adv.* —**fresh´ness** *n.*

Fri·day (frī´dā) *n.* the sixth day of the week

friend (frend) *n.* a person whom one knows well and likes

fries (frīz) *present tense form of the verb* **fry**

fright (frīt) *n.* **1** sudden fear; alarm **2** something that looks so strange or ugly as to startle one [That old fur coat is a perfect *fright.*]

frost (frôst) *n.* **1** frozen dew or vapor in the form of white crystals [the *frost* on the ground] **2** cold weather that can freeze things [*Frost* in the spring may damage fruit trees.]

frown (froun) *v.* to wrinkle the forehead and draw the eyebrows together in anger, worry, or deep thought ◆*n.* a frowning or the look one has in frowning

fro·zen (frōz´ən) *past participle of* **freeze** ◆*adj.* turned into or covered with ice [a *frozen* pond]

fry (frī) *v.* to cook in hot fat over direct heat [to *fry* eggs] —**fried, fry´ing, fries**

fume (fyo͞om) *n. often* **fumes**, *pl.* a gas, smoke, or vapor, especially if harmful or bad-smelling ◆*v.* **1** to give off fumes **2** to show that one is angry or irritated [He *fumed* at the long delay.] —**fumed, fum´ing**

Gg

garage (gər äzh´ *or* gər äj´) *n.* **1** a closed place where automobiles are sheltered **2** a place where automobiles are repaired

gar·den (gärd´n) *n.* a piece of ground where flowers, vegetables, etc., are grown ◆*v.* to take care of a garden —**gar·dener** (gärd´nər) *n.*

geese (gēs) *n. plural of* **goose**

gi·ant (jī´ənt) *n.* **1** an imaginary being that looks like a person but is many times larger and stronger **2** a person or thing that is especially large, strong, etc. [Einstein was a mental *giant.*]

give (giv) *v.* **1** to pass or hand over to another [*Give* me your coat, and I'll hang it up.] **2** to hand over to another to keep; make a gift of [My uncle *gave* a book to me for my birthday.] —**gave, giv´en, giv´ing** —**giv´er** *n.*

glass (glas) *n.* **1** a hard substance that breaks easily and that lets light through **2** a container made of glass and used for drinking —*pl.* **glass´es**

glide (glīd) *v.* to move along in a smooth and easy way [Skaters *glided* across the ice.] —**glid´ed, glid´ing**

glis·ten (glis´ən) *v.* to shine or sparkle with reflected light [The snow *glistened* in the sunlight.]

gloom·y (glo͞om´ē) *adj.* **1** dark or dim [a *gloomy* dungeon] **2** having or giving a feeling of deep sadness [a *gloomy* story] —**gloom´i·er, gloom´i·est**

glue (glo͞o) *n.* **1** a thick, sticky substance made by boiling animal hoofs and bones, used for sticking things together **2** any sticky substance like this ◆*v.* to stick together with glue —**glued, glu´ing** —**glue´y** *adj.*

gob·ble¹ (gäb´əl) *n.* the throaty sound made by a male turkey ◆*v.* to make this sound —**gob´bled, gob´bling**

gob·ble² (gäb´əl) *v.* to eat quickly and greedily —**gob´bled, gob´bling**

gone (gôn) *past participle of* **go** ◆*adj.* **1** moved away; departed **2** used up

good·bye *or* **good-bye** (go͝od bī´) *interj., n.* a word said when leaving someone; farewell [We said our *goodbyes* quickly and left.] —*pl.* **good·byes´** *or* **good-byes´**

good·ness (go͝od´nəs) *n.* the condition of being good ◆*interj.* an exclamation showing surprise [My *goodness! Goodness* me!]

a	ask, fat
ā	ape, date
ä	car, lot
e	elf, ten
ē	even, meet
i	is, hit
ī	ice, fire
ō	open, go
ô	law, horn
oi	oil, point
o͝o	look, pull
o͞o	ooze, tool
ou	out, crowd
u	up, cut
ʉ	fur, fern
ə	a in ago
	e in agent
	e in father
	i in unity
	o in collect
	u in focus
ch	chin, arch
ŋ	ring, singer
sh	she, dash
th	thin, truth
th	then, father
zh	s in pleasure

goose (g$\overline{oo}$s) **n.** a swimming bird that is like a duck but has a larger body and a longer neck; especially, the female of this bird —*pl.* **geese**

grape (grāp) **n.** a small round fruit, usually purple, red, or green, that grows in bunches on a woody vine —*pl.* **grapes**

grapes

graph (graf) **n.** a chart or diagram that shows the changes taking place in something, by the use of connected lines, a curve, etc. [a *graph* showing how sales figures vary during the year]

grate¹ (grāt) **v.** to grind into small bits or shreds by rubbing against a rough surface [to *grate* cabbage] **—grat´ed, grat´ing**

grate² (grāt) **n.** **1** a frame of metal bars for holding fuel, as in a fireplace or furnace **2** a framework of bars set in a window or door; grating

great (grāt) **adj.** **1** much above the average in size, degree, power, etc.; bit or very big; much or very much [the *Great* Lakes; a *great* distance; *great* pain] **2** very important; noted; remarkable [a *great* composer; a *great* discovery] **3** older or younger by a generation: *used in words formed with a hyphen* [my *great*-aunt; my *great*-niece] **—great´ly adv. —great´ness n.**

greet (grēt) **v.** to meet and speak to with polite and friendly words; to welcome [Our host *greeted* us with a warm "Hello!"] **—greet´ed, greet´ing**

grind (grīnd) **v.** **1** to crush into tiny bits or into powder [The miller *grinds* grain between millstones.] **2** to sharpen or smooth by rubbing against a rough surface [to *grind* a knife] **3** to press down or rub together harshly or with a grating sound [She *ground* her teeth in anger.] **—ground, grind´ing**

group (gr$\overline{oo}$p) **n.** a number of persons or things gathered together ◆**v.** to gather together into a group [*Group* yourselves in a circle.]

half (haf) **n.** either of the two equal parts of something [Five is *half* of ten.] —*pl.* **halves** ◆**adj.** being either of the two equal parts [a *half* gallon]

hard·ly (härd´lē) **adv.** only just; almost not [I can *hardly* tell them apart.]

harm (härm) **n.** **1** damage or hurt [Too much rain can do *harm* to crops.] **2** wrong; evil [I meant no *harm* by my remark.] ◆**v.** to do harm to; hurt or damage [Some cleaning fluids can *harm* the skin.]

has·n't (haz´ənt) **contraction** has not

hatch (hach) **v.** to come forth from the egg [Our chicks *hatched* this morning.]

haul (hôl) **v.** **1** to move by pulling; drag or tug [We *hauled* the boat up on the beach.] **2** to carry by wagon, truck, etc. [He *hauls* steel for a large company.] ◆**n.** the distance that something is hauled [It's a long *haul* to town.]

have·n't (hav´ənt) **contraction** have not

health (helth) **n.** the condition of being well in body and mind; freedom from sickness

hear (hir) **v.** **1** to receive sound through the ears [I *hear* music. Pat doesn't *hear* well.] **2** to listen to; pay attention [*Hear* what I tell you.] **—heard** (hʉrd), **hear´ing**

heav·y (hev´ē) **adj.** hard to lift or move because of its weight; weighing very much [a *heavy* load] **—heav´i·er, heav´i·est —heav´i·ly adv. —heav´i·ness n.**

help (help) **v.** **1** to give or do something that is needed or useful; make things easier for; aid; assist [We *helped* our poor relatives. *Help* me lift this.] **2** to make better; give relief to; remedy [This medicine will *help* your cold.] ◆**n.** the act of helping or a thing that helps; aid; assistance [Your advice was a great *help*.] **—help´er**

here (hir) *adv.* at or in this place [Who lives *here*?] ◆*interj.* a word called out to get attention, answer a roll call, etc. ◆*n.* this place [Let's get out of *here*.]

he·ro (hir′ō) *n.* 1 a person, especially a man or boy, who is looked up to for having done something brave or noble [He became a *hero* when he saved his family from a burning house. Washington was the *hero* of the American Revolution.] 2 the most important man in a novel, play, etc., especially if he is good or noble —*pl.* **he′roes**

he's (hēz) *contraction* 1 he is 2 he has

high·way (hī′wā) *n.* a main road

hob·by (häb′ē) *n.* something that one likes to do for pleasure in one's spare time [Her *hobby* is collecting stamps.] —*pl.* **hob′bies**

hock·ey (häk′ē) *n.* a game played on ice, in which the players wear ice skates and use curved sticks to try to drive or push a rubber disk into the other team's goal

hol·i·day (häl′ə dā′) *n.* a day on which most people do not have to work, often one set aside by law [Thanksgiving is a *holiday* in all states.]

hon·ey (hun′ē) *n.* 1 a thick, sweet, yellow syrup that bees make from the nectar of flowers and store in honeycombs 2 sweet one; darling: used in talking to someone dear to one [How are you, *honey*?]

hon·or (än′ər) *n.* 1 great respect given because of worth, noble deeds, high rank, etc. [to pay *honor* to the geniuses of science] 2 something done or given as a sign of respect [Madame Curie received many *honors* for her work.] 3 good name or reputation [You must uphold the *honor* of the family.] 4 a being true to what is right, honest, etc. [Her sense of *honor* kept her from cheating.] ◆*v.* to have or show great respect for [America *honors* the memory of Lincoln. *Honor* your father and your mother.] ◆*adj.* of or showing honor [an *honor* roll]

hope (hōp) *n.* a feeling that what one wants will happen [We gave up *hope* of being rescued.] ◆*v.* 1 to have hope; want and expect [I *hope* to see you soon.] 2 to want to believe [I *hope* I didn't overlook anybody.] —**hoped, hop′ing**

hour (our) *n.* 1 any of the 24 equal parts of a day; 60 minutes 2 a particular time [At what *hour* shall we meet?]

how's (houz) *contraction* 1 how is 2 how has 3 how does

huge (hyōōj) *adj.* very large; immense [the *huge* trunk of the redwood tree] —**huge′ly** *adv.* —**huge′ness** *n.*

hu·man (hyōō′mən) *adj.* that is a person or that has to do with people in general [a *human* being; *human* affairs] ◆*n.* a person: *some people still prefer the full phrase* **human being**

hum·ble (hum′bəl) *adj.* knowing one's own weaknesses and faults; not proud or bold; modest or meek [He became *humble* and asked her to forgive him.] —**hum′bler, hum′blest**

hun·gry (huŋ′grē) *adj.* 1 wanting or needing food [Cold weather makes me *hungry*.] 2 having a strong desire; eager [*hungry* for praise] —**hun′gri·er, hun′gri·est** —**hun′gri·ly** *adv.* —**hun′gri·ness** *n.*

hunt·er (hunt′ər) *n.* a person who hunts

hur·ried (hur′ēd) *adj.* done or acting in a hurry; hasty [We ate a *hurried* lunch.] —**hur′ried·ly** *adv.*

hurt (hurt) *v.* 1 to cause pain or injury to; wound [The fall *hurt* my leg.] 2 to have pain [My head *hurts*.] 3 to harm or damage in some way [Water won't *hurt* this tabletop.] —**hurt, hurt′ing** ◆*n.* pain, injury, or harm [Warm water will ease the *hurt*.]

a	ask, fat
ā	ape, date
ä	car, lot
e	elf, ten
ē	even, meet
i	is, hit
ī	ice, fire
ō	open, go
ô	law, horn
oi	oil, point
ōō	look, pull
ōō	ooze, tool
ou	out, crowd
u	up, cut
ʉ	fur, fern
ə	a in ago
	e in agent
	e in father
	i in unity
	o in collect
	u in focus
ch	chin, arch
ŋ	ring, singer
sh	she, dash
th	thin, truth
th	then, father
zh	s in pleasure

Ii

jog

ice (īs) *n.* water frozen solid by cold [Water turns to *ice* at 0°C.] ◆*v.* **1** to change into ice; freeze [The lake *iced* over.] **2** to cover with icing, or frosting [to *ice* a cake] —**iced, ic´ing**

I'd (īd) *contraction* **1** I had **2** I would **3** I should

I'll (īl) *contraction* **1** I shall **2** I will

inch (inch) *n.* a unit for measuring length, equal to 1/12 foot; one inch equals 2.54 centimeters —*pl.* **inch´es** ◆*v.* to move a little at a time [Lou *inched* along the narrow ledge.]

in·side (in´sīd´) *n.* the side or part that is within; interior [Wash the windows on the *inside*.] ◆*adj.* on or in the inside; internal; indoor [*inside* work; an *inside* page]

in·stead (in sted´) *adv.* in place of the other; as a substitute [If you have no cream, use milk *instead*.]

is·land (ī´lənd) *n.* a piece of land that is smaller than a continent and is surrounded by water

is·n't (iz´ənt) *contraction* is not

itch (ich) *v.* to have a tickling feeling on the skin that makes one want to scratch; also, to cause to have this feeling [The wool shirt *itches* my skin.] ◆*n.* an itching feeling on the skin

its (its) *pron.* of it or done by it: *the possessive form of* **it**, *thought of as an adjective* [Give the cat *its* dinner. The frost had done *its* damage.]

I've (īv) *contraction* I have

Jj

jail (jāl) *n.* a building where people are locked up while they are waiting for a trial or serving a short sentence

jog (jäg) *v.* to move along slowly or steadily, but with a jolting motion —**jogged, jog´ging** ◆*n.* a jogging pace; trot —**jog´ger**

join (join) *v.* **1** to bring together; connect; fasten [We *joined* hands and stood in a circle.] **2** to become a part or member of [Paula has *joined* our club.] **3** to take part along with others [*Join* in the game.]

joke (jōk) *n.* anything said or done to get a laugh, as a funny story ◆*v.* to tell or play jokes —**joked, jok´ing** —**jok´ing·ly** *adv.*

Kk

kill (kil) *v.* **1** to cause the death of; make die; slay **2** to put an end to; destroy or ruin [Her defeat *killed* all our hopes.] **3** to make time pass in doing unimportant things [an hour to *kill* before my train leaves] ◆*n.* **1** the act of killing [to be in at the *kill*] **2** an animal or animals killed [the lion's *kill*] —**kill´er**

kind¹ (kīnd) *n.* sort or variety [all *kinds* of books]

kind² (kīnd) *adj.* **1** always ready to help others and do good; friendly, gentle, generous, sympathetic, etc. **2** showing goodness, generosity, sympathy, etc. [*kind* deeds; *kind* regards]

knee (nē) *n.* the joint between the thigh and the lower leg

knew (nōō *or* nyōō) *past tense of* **know**

knife (nīf) *n.* a tool having a flat, sharp blade set in a handle, used for cutting —*pl.* **knives** ◆*v.* to cut or stab with a knife —**knifed, knif´ing**

knight (nīt) *n.* a man in the Middle Ages who was given a military rank of honor after serving as a page and squire: knights were supposed to be gallant and brave ◆*v.* to give the rank of knight to

knit (nit) *v.* **1** to make by looping yarn or thread together with special needles [to *knit* a scarf] —**knit´ted** or **knit, knit´ting**

knives (nīvz) *n.* *plural of* **knife**

knock (näk) **v. 1** to hit as with the fist; especially, to rap on a door [Who is *knocking*?] to hit and cause to fall [The dog *knocked* down the papergirl.] ◆**n.** a hard, loud blow, as with the fist; rap, as on a door

knot (nät) **n. 1** a lump, as in a string or ribbon, formed by a loop or a tangle drawn tight **2** a fastening made by tying together parts or pieces of string, rope, etc. [Sailors make a variety of *knots*.] ◆**v. 1** to tie or fasten with a knot; make a knot in **2** to become tangled —**knot´ted, knot´ting**

know (nō) **v. 1** to be sure of or have the facts about [Do you *know* why grass is green? She *knows* the law.] **2** to have in one's mind or memory [The actress *knows* her lines.] **3** to be acquainted with [I *know* your brother well.] —**knew, known, know´ing**

Ll

lack (lak) **n. 1** the condition of not having enough; shortage [*Lack* of money forced him to return home.] **2** the thing that is needed [Our most serious *lack* was fresh water.] ◆**v.** to be without or not have enough; need [The soil *lacks* nitrogen.]

la·dy (lā´dē) **n.** a woman, especially one who is polite and refined and has a sense of honor —*pl.* **la´dies** ◆**adj.** that is a woman; female [a *lady* barber]

large (lärj) **adj.** of great size or amount; big [a *large* house; a *large* sum of money] —**larg´er, larg´est** ◆**adv.** in a large way [Don't write so *large*.] —**large´ness n.**

late·ly (lāt´lē) **adv.** just before this time; not long ago; recently

laugh (laf) **v.** to make a series of quick sounds with the voice that show one is amused or happy or, sometimes, that show scorn: one usually smiles or grins when laughing ◆**n.** the act or sound of laughing

law (lô) **n.** all the rules that tell people what they must or must not do, made by the government of a city, state, nation, etc. [the *law* of the land]

lawn (lôn) **n.** ground covered with grass that is cut short, as around a house

leaf (lēf) **n. 1** any of the flat, green parts growing from the stem of a plant or tree **2** a sheet of paper in a book [Each side of a *leaf* is a page.] —*pl.* **leaves** —**leaf´less adj.**

lean (lēn) **v.** to bend or slant so as to rest upon something [Pedro *leaned* against the desk.] —**leaned** or **leant, lean´ing**

learn (lurn) **v. 1** to get some knowledge or skill, as by studying or being taught [I have *learned* to knit. Some people never *learn* from experience.] **2** to find out about something; come to know [When did you *learn* of his illness?] **3** to fix in the mind; memorize [*Learn* this poem by tomorrow.] —**learned** (lurnd) or **learnt** (lurnt), **learn´ing**

least (lēst) **adj.** smallest in size, amount, or importance [I haven't the *least* interest in the matter.] ◆**adv.** in the smallest amount or degree [I was *least* impressed by the music.] ◆**n.** the smallest in amount, degree, etc. [The *least* you can do is apologize. I'm not in the *least* interested.]

leave (lēv) **v.** to go away or go from [Rosa *left* early. Jose *leaves* the house at 8:00.] —**left, leav´ing**

leaves (lēvz) **n.** *plural of* **leaf**

left¹ (left) **adj.** on or to the side that is toward the west when one faces north [the *left* hand; a *left* turn] ◆**n.** the left side [Forks are placed at the *left* of the plate.] ◆**adv.** on or toward the left hand or side [Turn *left* here.]

left² (left) *past tense and past participle of* **leave**

knot

leaf

a	ask, fat
ā	ape, date
ä	car, lot
e	elf, ten
ē	even, meet
i	is, hit
ī	ice, fire
ō	open, go
ô	law, horn
σi	oil, point
σσ	look, pull
σ̄σ̄	ooze, tool
σu	out, crowd
u	up, cut
ʉ	fur, fern
ə	a in ago
	e in agent
	e in father
	i in unity
	o in collect
	u in focus
ch	chin, arch
ŋ	ring, singer
sh	she, dash
th	thin, truth
th	then, father
zh	s in pleasure

167

loaf

lev·el (lev'əl) *adj.* with no part higher than any other part; flat and even [a *level* plane] ◆*n.* a small tube of liquid in a frame that is placed on a surface to see if the surface is level: a bubble in the liquid moves to the center of the tube when the frame is level ◆*v.* to make level or flat [to *level* ground with a bulldozer] —**lev'eled** or **lev'elled, lev'el·ing** or **lev'el·ling**

lie¹ (lī) *v.* **1** to stretch one's body in a flat position along the ground, a bed, etc. **2** to be in a flat position; rest [A book is *lying* on the table.] —**lay, lain, ly'ing**

lie² (lī) *n.* something said that is not true, especially if it is said on purpose to fool or trick someone ◆*v.* to tell a lie; say what is not true —**lied, ly'ing**

life (līf) *n.* **1** the quality of plants and animals that makes it possible for them to take in food, grow, produce others of their kind, etc., and that makes them different from rocks, water, etc. [Death is the loss of *life*.] **2** a living thing; especially, a human being [The crash took six *lives*.] **3** the time that a person or thing is alive or lasts [Her *life* has just begun. What is the *life* of a batter?] —*pl.* **lives**

light¹ (līt) *n.* **1** brightness or radiance [the *light* of a candle; the *light* of love in his eyes] **2** something that gives light, as a lamp [Turn off the *light*.] **3** a flame or spark to start something burning [a *light* for a pipe] —**light'ness** ◆*adj.* **1** having light; not dark [It's getting *light* outside.] **2** having a pale color; fair [*light* hair] ◆*adv.* not brightly; in a pale way [a *light* green dress] ◆*v.* to set on fire or catch fire; burn [to *light* a match; the candle *lighted* at once] —**light'ed** or **lit, light'ing**

light² (līt) *adj.* having little weight, especially for its size; not heavy [a *light* cargo; a *light* suit]

lit·tle (lit'l) *adj.* small in size; not large or big [a *little* house] —**lit'tler** or **less** or **less'er, lit'tlest** or **least** ◆*adv.* to a small degree; not very much [She is a *little* better.] —**less, least** ◆*n.* a small amount [Have a *little* of this cake.] —**lit'tle·ness** *n.*

live¹ (liv) *v.* **1** to have life; be alive [No one *lives* forever.] **2** to make one's home; reside [We *live* on a farm.] —**lived, liv'ing**

live² (līv) *adj.* **1** having life; not dead **2** that is broadcast while it is taking place; not photographed or recorded [a *live* television or radio program]

liv·ing (liv'iŋ) *adj.* having life; alive; not dead ◆*n.* **1** the fact of being alive **2** the means of supporting oneself or one's family [He makes a *living* selling shoes.]

load (lōd) *n.* something that is carried or to be carried at one time [a heavy *load* on his back] ◆*v.* to put something to be carried into or upon a carrier [to *load* a bus with passengers; to *load* groceries into a cart] —**load'er** *n.*

loaf (lōf) *n.* **1** a portion of bread baked in one piece, usually oblong in shape **2** any food baked in this shape [a meat *loaf*] —*pl.* **loaves**

long¹ (lôŋ) *adj.* **1** measuring much from end to end or from beginning to end; not short [a *long* board; a *long* trip; a *long* wait] **2** taking a longer time to say than other sounds [The "a" in "cave" and the "i" in "hide" are *long*.] ◆*adv.* for a long time [Don't be gone *long*.]

long² (lôŋ) *v.* to want very much; feel a strong desire for [We *long* to go home.]

loose (lōōs) *adj.* **1** not tied or held back; free [a *loose* end of wire] **2** not tight or firmly fastened on or in something [*loose* clothing; a *loose* table leg] ◆*adv.* in a loose way [My coat hangs *loose*.] —**loose'ly** *adv.* —**loose'ness** *n.*

lose (lōōz) *v.* **1** to put, leave, or drop, so as to be unable to find; misplace; mislay [He *lost* his keys somewhere.] **2** to fail to win; be defeated [We *lost* the football game.] —**lost, los'ing**

lost (lôst) *past tense and past participle of* **lose** ➛*adj.* that is mislaid, missing, destroyed, defeated, wasted, etc. [a *lost* hat; a *lost* child; a *lost* ship; a *lost* cause; *lost* time]

loud (loud) *adj.* **1** strong in sound; not soft or quiet [a *loud* noise; a *loud* bell] **2** noisy [a *loud* party] ➛*adv.* in a loud way —**loud´ly** —**loud´ness** *n.*

love·ly (luv´lē) *adj.* **1** very pleasing in looks or character; beautiful [a *lovely* person] **2** very enjoyable: *used only in everyday talk* [We had a *lovely* time.] —**love´li·er, love´li·est** —**love´li·ness** *n.*

loy·al (loi´əl) *adj.* **1** faithful to one's country [a *loyal* citizen] **2** faithful to one's family, duty, beliefs, etc. [a *loyal* friend; a *loyal* member] —**loy´al·ly** *adv.*

Mm

mad (mad) *adj.* **1** angry [Don't be *mad* at us for leaving.] **2** crazy; insane —**mad´der, mad´dest**

made (mād) *past tense and past participle of* **make** ➛*adj.* built; put together; formed [a well-*made* house]

mag·ic (maj´ik) *n.* **1** the use of charms, spells, and rituals that are supposed to make things happen in an unnatural way [In fairy tales, *magic* is used to work miracles.] **2** the skill of doing puzzling tricks by moving the hands so fast as to fool those watching and by using boxes with false bottoms, hidden strings, etc.; sleight of hand ➛*adj.* of or as if by magic

mag·ni·fy (mag´nə fī) *v.* to make something seem larger or greater than it really is [This lens *magnifies* an object to ten times its size.] — **mag´ni·fies, mag´ni·fied, mag´ni·fy·ing**

maid (mād) *n.* **1** a maiden **2** a girl or woman servant

mail (māl) *n.* **1** letters, packages, etc., carried and delivered by a post office **2** the system of picking up and delivering letters, papers, etc.; postal system [Send it by *mail.*] ➛*adj.* having to do with or carrying mail [a *mail* truck] ☆➛*v.* to send by mail; place in a mailbox —**mail´a·ble** *adj.*

main (mān) *adj.* first in size or importance; chief; principal [the *main* characters in a movie]

make (māk) *v.* **1** to bring into being; build, create, produce, put together, etc. [to *make* a dress; to *make* a fire; to *make* plans; to *make* noise] **2** to do, perform, carry on, etc. [to *make* a right turn; to *make* a speech] —**made, mak´ing**

man (man) *n.* **1** an adult male human being **2** any human being; person ["…that all *men* are created equal…"] **3** the human race; mankind [*man's* conquest of space] —*pl.* **men**

mark (märk) *n.* **1** a spot, stain, scratch, dent, etc., made on a surface **2** a printed or written sign or label [punctuation *marks*; a trade*mark*] **3** a grade or rating [a *mark* of B in spelling] ➛*v.* **1** to make a mark or marks on **2** to draw or write [*Mark* your name on your gym shoes.] **3** to give a grade to [to *mark* test papers]

mar·ry (mer´ē) *v.* **1** to join a man and a woman as husband and wife [A ship's captain may *marry* people at sea.] **2** to take as one's husband or wife [John Alden *married* Priscilla.] —**mar´ried, mar´ry·ing**

may (mā) *a helping verb used with other verbs and meaning:* **1** to be possible or likely [It *may* rain.] **2** to be allowed or have permission [You *may* go.] **3** to be able to as a result [Be quiet so that we *may* hear.] **4** used in an exclamation to express a wish [*May* you win!] —**might**

may·be (mā´bē) *adv.* it may be; perhaps

mean·ing (mēn´iŋ) *n.* what is supposed to be understood [She repeated the words to make her *meaning* clear.]

mail

a	ask, fat
ā	ape, date
ä	car, lot
e	elf, ten
ē	even, meet
i	is, hit
ī	ice, fire
ō	open, go
ô	law, horn
oi	oil, point
oo	look, pull
oo	ooze, tool
ou	out, crowd
u	up, cut
ʉ	fur, fern
ə	a in ago
	e in agent
	e in father
	i in unity
	o in collect
	u in focus
ch	chin, arch
ŋ	ring, singer
sh	she, dash
th	thin, truth
th	then, father
zh	s in pleasure

mel·o·dy (mel′ə dē) **n. 1** an arrangement of musical tones in a series so as to form a tune; often, the main tune in the harmony of a musical piece [The *melody* is played by the oboes.] **2** any pleasing series of sounds [a *melody* sung by birds] —*pl.* **mel′o·dies**

melt (melt) **v. 1** to change from a solid to a liquid, as by heat [The snow *melted* in the sun.] **2** to dissolve [The cough drop *melted* in my mouth.]

men (men) **n.** *plural of* **man**

mice (mīs) **n.** *plural of* **mouse**

might¹ (mīt) *past tense of* **may**

might² (mīt) **n.** great strength, force, or power [Pull with all your *might*.]

mile (mīl) **n.** a standard measure of length, equal of 5,280 feet or 1,760 yards or 1.6093 kilometers

mix (miks) **v.** to put, stir, or come together to form a single, blended thing [*Mix* red and yellow paint to get orange.] —**mixed, mix′ing** ◆*n.* a mixture —*pl.* **mix′es**

Monday (mun′dā) **n.** the second day of the week

mon·ey (mun′ē) **n.** coins of gold, silver, or other metal, or paper bills to take the place of these, issued by a government for use in buying and selling —*pl.* **mon′eys** or **mon′ies**

mood (mood) **n.** the way one feels; frame of mind [She's in a happy *mood* today.]

moon·light (moon′līt) **n.** the light of the moon

morn·ing (môrn′iŋ) **n.** the early part of the day, from midnight to noon or, especially, from dawn to noon

most·ly (mōst′lē) **adv.** mainly; chiefly

moth (môth *or* mäth) **n.** an insect similar to the butterfly, but usually smaller and less brightly colored and flying mostly at night —*pl.* **moths** (môthz *or* mäths)

mouse (mous) **n. 1** a small, gnawing animal found in houses and fields throughout the world. **2** a timid person —*pl.* **mice** (mīs) ☆**3** a small device moved by hand, as on a flat surface, so as to make the cursor move on a computer-terminal screen

mul·ti·ply (mul′tə plī′) **v. 1** to become more, greater, etc.; increase [Our troubles *multiplied*.] **2** to repeat a certain figure a certain number of times [If you *multiply* 10 by 4, or repeat 10 four times, you get the product 40.] —**mul′ti·plied′, mul′ti·ply′ing**

mu·sic (myoo′zik) **n. 1** the art of putting tones together in various melodies, rhythms, and harmonies to form compositions for singing or playing on instruments [She teaches *music*.] **2** any series of pleasing sounds [the *music* of birds]

must·n't (mus′ənt) **contraction** must not

mute (myoot) **adj.** not able to speak ◆*v.* to soften or muffle the sound of

nee·dle (nēd′əl) **n. 1** a small, slender piece of steel with a sharp point and a hole for thread, used for sewing **2** a short, slender piece of metal, often tipped with diamond, that moves in the grooves of a phonograph record to pick up the vibrations **3** the thin, pointed leaf of a pine, spruce, etc. **4** the sharp, very slender metal tube at the end of a hypodermic syringe

next (nekst) **adj.** coming just before or just after; nearest or closest [the *next* person in line; the *next* room; *next* Monday] ◆*adv.* **1** in the nearest place, time, etc. [She sits *next* to me in school. Please wait on me *next*.] **2** at the first chance after this [What should I do *next*?]

nice (nīs) **adj.** good, pleasant, agreeable, pretty, kind, polite, etc.: *used as a general word showing that one likes something* [a *nice* time; a *nice* dress; a *nice* neighbor] —**nic′er, nic′est** —**nice′ly adv.**

night (nīt) **n.** the time of darkness between sunset and sunrise ◆*adj.* of, for, or at night [*night* school]

nine (nīn) **n., adj.** one more than eight; the number 9

ninth (nīnth) *adj.* coming after eight others; 9th in order ◆*n.* one of nine equal parts of something; 1/9

note (nōt) *n.* **1** a word, phrase, or sentence written down to help one remember something one has heard, read, thought, etc. [The students kept *notes* on the lecture.] **2** a short letter **3** close attention; notice [Take *note* of what I say.] **4** a musical tone; also, the symbol for such a tone, showing how long it is to be sounded: where it is placed on the staff tells how high or low it is

noun (noun) *n.* a word that is the name of a person, thing, action, quality, etc.: a phrase or a clause can be used in a sentence as a noun ["Boy," "water," and "truth" are *nouns.*]

nurse (nɬrs) *n.* a person who has been trained to take care of sick people, help doctors, etc. ◆*v.* to take care of sick people, as a nurse does —**nursed, nurs´ing**

Oo

once (wuns) *adv.* **1** one time [We eat together *once* a week.] **2** at sometime in the past; formerly [They were *once* rich.] ◆*conj.* as soon as; whenever [*Once* the horse tires, it will quit.] ◆*n.* one time [I'll go this *once.*]

on·ly (ōn´lē) *adj.* without any other or others of the same kind; sole [the *only* suit I own; their *only* friends] ◆*adv.* and no other; and no more; just; merely [I have *only* fifty cents. Bite off *only* what you can chew.]

or·der (ôr´dər) *n.* **1** the way in which things are placed or follow one another; arrangement [The entries in this dictionary are in alphabetical *order.*] **2** a direction telling someone what to do, given by a person with authority; command [The general's *orders* were quickly obeyed.] **3** a request for something that one wants to buy or receive [Mail your *order* for flower seeds today.] ◆*v.* **1** to tell what to do; give an order to [The captain *ordered* the troops to

charge.] **2** to ask for something one wants to buy or receive [Please *order* some art supplies for the class.]

our (our) *pron.* of us or done by us: *this possessive form of* **we** *is used before a noun and thought of as an adjective* [*our* car; *our* work]

own·er (ōn´ər) *n.* a person who owns something

ox (äks) *n.* any animal of a group that chew their cud and have cloven hoofs, including the buffalo, bison, etc. —*pl.* **ox·en** (äks´ən)

Pp

pack (pak) *n.* a bundle of things that is tied or wrapped [a hiker's *pack*] ◆*v.* **1** to tie or wrap together in a bundle [I *packed* books at the book sale.] **2** to put things together in a box, trunk, or suitcase for carrying or storing [to *pack* a suitcase]

paid (pād) *past tense and past participle of* **pay**

paint (pānt) *n.* a mixture of coloring matter and water, oil, or some other liquid used to make a picture or to coat a surface in order to color or protect it ◆*v.* to use paint [She *paints* as a hobby.]

pair (per) *n.* **1** two things of the same kind that are used together; set of two [a *pair* of skates] **2** a single thing with two parts that are used together [a *pair* of eyeglasses; a *pair* of pants] ◆*v.* to arrange in or form a pair or pairs; match

pa·per (pā´pər) *n.* **1** a thin material in sheets, made from wood pulp, rags, etc., and used to write or print on, to wrap or decorate with, etc. **2** a single sheet of this material **3** something written or printed on paper, as an essay, report, etc. [The teacher is grading a set of *papers.*]

pare (per) *v.* to cut or trim away the rind or covering of something; peel [to *pare* a potato; to *pare* the bark from a tree] —**pared, par´ing**

a	ask, fat
ā	ape, date
ä	car, lot
e	elf, ten
ē	even, meet
i	is, hit
ī	ice, fire
ō	open, go
ô	law, horn
oi	oil, point
ʊ	look, pull
oo	ooze, tool
ou	out, crowd
u	up, cut
ɬ	fur, fern
ə	a in ago
	e in agent
	e in father
	i in unity
	o in collect
	u in focus
ch	chin, arch
ŋ	ring, singer
sh	she, dash
th	thin, truth
th	then, father
zh	s in pleasure

pie

par·ty (pär′tē) **n.** **1** a gathering of people to have a good time [a birthday *party*] **2** a group of people working or acting together [a hunting *party*] —*pl.* **par′ties**

pass (pas) **v.** to go by, beyond, over, or through [I *pass* your house every day.] —**passed, pass′ing** ◆**n.** **1** the act of passing; passage **2** a free ticket [We got two *passes* to the movies.] —*pl.* **pass′es**

past (past) **adj.** gone by; ended; over [What is *past* is finished.] ◆**n.** the time that has gone by [That's all in the *past*.] ◆**prep.** later than or farther than; beyond [ten minutes *past* two; *past* the city limits]

patch (pach) **n.** **1** a piece of cloth, metal, etc., put on to mend a hole, tear, or worn spot **2** a bandage put on a wound or a pad worn over an injured eye **3** an area or spot [*patches* of blue sky] ◆**v.** to put a patch or patches on [to *patch* the worn elbows of a coat]

pay (pā) **v.** to give money to for products or services [Did you *pay* the cab driver?] —**paid, pay′ing**

peach (pēch) **n.** a round, juicy, pinkish-yellow fruit with a fuzzy skin and a rough pit —*pl.* **peach′es**

pear (per) **n.** a soft, juicy fruit, often yellow or green, that is round at one end and narrows toward the stem

peo·ple (pē′pəl) **n.** human beings; persons

per·son (pur′sən) **n.** a human being; man, woman, or child [every *person* in this room]

☆**phone** (fōn) **n., v.** *a shorter word for* **telephone**: *used only in everyday talk* —**phoned, phon′ing**

pick¹ (pik) **n.** a heavy metal tool with a pointed head, used for breaking up rock, soil, etc.

pick² (pik) **v.** **1** to choose or select [The judges *picked* the winner.] **2** to scratch or dig at with the fingers or with something pointed [to *pick* the teeth with a toothpick] **3** to pluck or gather with the fingers or hands [to *pick* flowers] ◆**n.** the act of choosing or the thing chosen; choice [Take your *pick* of these books.] —**pick′er n.**

pie (pī) **n.** a dish with a filling usually made of fruit or meat baked in a pastry crust —*pl.* **pies**

pinch (pinch) **v.** to squeeze between a finger and the thumb or between two surfaces [He gently *pinched* the baby's cheek. She *pinched* her finger in the door.] ◆**n.** **1** a pinching; squeeze; nip [a *pinch* on the arm] **2** the amount that can be picked up between the finger and thumb [a *pinch* of salt]

pint (pīnt) **n.** a unit of volume that is equal to half a quart

pitch (pich) **v.** **1** to throw or toss [*Pitch* the newspaper on the porch.] **2** to set up; make ready for use [to *pitch* a tent] **3** to slope downward [The roof *pitches* sharply.] ◆**n.** **1** anything pitched or thrown [The wild *pitch* hit the batter.] **2** the highness or lowness of a musical sound

place (plās) **n.** **1** a space taken up or used by a person or thing [Please take your *places*.] **2** a house, apartment, etc., where one lives [Visit me at my *place*.] **3** rank or position, especially in a series [I finished the race in fifth *place*.] ◆**v.** **1** to put in a certain place, position, etc. [*Place* the pencil on the desk.] **2** to finish in a certain position in a contest [Lynn *placed* sixth in the race.] —**placed, plac′ing**

plan (plan) **n.** **1** a method or way of doing something that has been thought out ahead of time [vacation *plans*] **2** a drawing that shows how the parts of a building or piece of ground are arranged [floor *plans* of a house; a *plan* of the battlefield] ◆**v.** **1** to think out a way of making or doing something [They *planned* their escape carefully.] **2** to make a drawing or diagram of beforehand [An architect is *planning* our new school.] **3** to have in mind; intend [I *plan* to visit Hawaii soon.] —**planned, plan′ning**

plane (plān) **n.** *a short form of* **airplane**

plant (plant) *n.* **1** any living thing that cannot move about by itself, has no sense organs, and usually makes its own food by photosynthesis [Trees, shrubs, and vegetables are *plants*.] **2** the machinery, buildings, etc., of a factory or business ◆*v.* to put into the ground so that it will grow [to *plant* corn]

play (plā) *v.* **1** to have fun; amuse oneself [children *playing* in the sand] **2** to do in fun [to *play* a joke on a friend] **3** to take part in a game or sport [to *play* golf] **4** to perform music on [He *plays* the piano.] **5** to give out sounds: said of a phonograph, tape recorder, etc. ◆*n.* **1** something done just for fun or to amuse oneself; recreation [She has little time for *play*.] **2** fun; joking [Jan said it in *play*.] **3** the playing of a game [Rain halted *play*.] **4** a story that is acted out, as on a stage, on radio or television, etc.; drama

play·ful (plā′fəl) *adj.* **1** fond of play or fun; lively; frisky [a *playful* puppy] **2** said or done in fun; joking [She gave her brother a *playful* shove.] —**play′ful·ly** *adv.* —**play′ful·ness** *n.*

please (plēz) *v.* **1** to give pleasure to; satisfy [Few things *please* me more than a good book.] **2** to be kind enough to: *used in asking for something politely* [*Please* pass the salt.] **3** to wish or desire; like [Do as you *please*.] —**pleased, pleas′ing**

plen·ty (plen′tē) *n.* a supply that is large enough; all that is needed [We have *plenty* of help.]

point (point) *n.* **1** a position or place; location [the *point* where the roads meet] **2** a dot in printing or writing [a decimal *point*] **3** a unit used in measuring or scoring [A touchdown is worth six *points*.] **4** a sharp end [the *point* of a needle] **5** an important or main idea or fact [the *point* of a joke] ◆*v.* to aim one's finger [He *pointed* to the book he wanted.]

pol·ish (päl′ish) *v.* to make smooth and bright or shiny, usually by rubbing [to *polish* a car with wax] ◆*n.* **1** brightness or shine on a surface [a wood floor with a fine *polish*] **2** a substance used for polishing [shoe *polish*] —*pl.* **pol′ish·es**

po·lite (pə līt′) *adj.* having or showing good manners; thoughtful of others; courteous [a *polite* note of thanks] —**po·lite′ly** *adv.* —**po·lite′ness** *n.*

pool¹ (pool) *n.* **1** a small pond **2** a puddle **3** *a shorter form of* **swimming pool**

pool² (pool) *n.* a game of billiards played on a table, called a **pool table**, having six pockets into which the balls are knocked

po·ta·to (pə tāt′ō) *n.* a plant whose tuber, or thick, starchy underground stem, is used as a vegetable —*pl.* **po·ta′toes**

pound¹ (pound) *n.* a unit of weight, equal to 16 ounces in avoirdupois weight or 12 ounces in troy weight: one pound avoirdupois equals 453.59 grams

pound² (pound) *v.* **1** to hit with many heavy blows; hit hard [to *pound* on a door] **2** to beat in a heavy way; throb [Her heart *pounded* from the exercise.] ◆*n.* a hard blow or the sound of it

pound³ (pound) *n.* a closed-in place for keeping animals, especially stray ones [a dog *pound*]

pour (pôr) *v.* to let flow in a steady stream [He *poured* the milk into the glass.]

pow·er (pou′ər) *n.* **1** ability to do or act [Lobsters have the *power* to grow new claws.] **2** strength or force [the *power* of a boxer's blows] **3** force or energy that can be put to work [electric *power*] **4** the ability to control others; authority [the *power* of the law] ◆*adj.* worked by electricity or other kind of power [a *power* saw]

pray (prā) *v.* **1** to talk or recite a set of words to God in worship or in asking for something **2** to beg or ask for seriously ["*Pray* tell me" means "I beg you to tell me."]

plant

a	ask, fat
ā	ape, date
ä	car, lot
e	elf, ten
ē	even, meet
i	is, hit
ī	ice, fire
ō	open, go
ò	law, horn
oi	oil, point
ōō	look, pull
o͞o	ooze, tool
ou	out, crowd
u	up, cut
ʉ	fur, fern
ə	a in ago
	e in agent
	e in father
	i in unity
	o in collect
	u in focus
ch	chin, arch
ŋ	ring, singer
sh	she, dash
th	thin, truth
th	then, father
zh	s in pleasure

puppy

pre·pare (pri par´) **v.** to make or get ready [We *prepared* for the test.] —**pre·pared´, pre·par´ing**

pret·ty (prit´ē) **adj.** pleasant to look at or hear, especially in a delicate, dainty, or graceful way [a *pretty* girl; a *pretty* voice; a *pretty* garden] —**pret´ti·er, pret´ti·est** ◆**adv.** somewhat; rather [I'm *pretty* tired.] ◆**v.** to make pretty [She *prettied* up her room.] —**pret´tied, pret´ty·ing** —**pret´ti·ly adv.** —**pret´ti·ness n.**

proud (proud) **adj.** **1** having proper respect for oneself, one's work, one's family, etc. [He is too *proud* to ask for help.] **2** thinking too highly of oneself; conceited; vain or haughty [They are too *proud* to say hello to us.] **3** feeling or causing pride or pleasure [his *proud* mother; a *proud* moment] —**proud´ly adv.**

pry (prī) **v.** to raise or move with a lever or a crowbar [Let's *pry* up the top of the crate.] —**pried, pry´ing** ◆**n.** a lever or crowbar —*pl.* **pries**

pup·py (pup´ē) **n.** a young dog —*pl.* **pup´pies**

pur·ple (pur´pəl) **n.** **1** a color that is a mixture of red and blue **2** crimson clothing worn long ago by royalty and high officials ◆**adj.** of or having to do with the color purple

purse (purs) **n.** a small container for carrying money [a coin *purse*]

push (poosh) **v.** **1** to press against so as to move; shove [to *push* a stalled car; to *push* a stake into the ground] **2** to urge the use, sale, etc., of [The company is *pushing* its new product.] ◆**n.** the act of pushing; a shove or thrust [One hard *push* opened the door.]

Qq

quite (kwīt) **adv.** **1** completely; entirely [I haven't *quite* finished eating.] **2** really; truly [You are *quite* a musician.] **3** very or somewhat [It's *quite* warm outside.]

Rr

rac·coon (ra koon´) **n.** a furry animal having a long tail with black rings and black face markings that look like a mask

race (rās) **n.** a contest, as among runners, swimmers, cars, boats, etc., to see who can go fastest ◆**v.** **1** to take part in a race [How many planes are *racing*?] **2** to have a race with [I'll *race* you to the corner.] **3** to go very fast [Her eye *raced* over the page.] —**raced, rac´ing**

rain (rān) **n.** **1** water that falls to the earth in drops formed from the moisture in the air. **2** the falling of such drops; a shower [Sunshine followed the *rain*.] ◆**v.** to fall as rain [It is *raining*.]

raise (rāz) **v.** **1** to cause to rise; lift [*Raise* your hand if you have a question. *Raise* the window.] **2** to make larger, greater, higher, louder, etc. [to *raise* prices; to *raise* one's voice] **3** to bring up; take care of; support [to *raise* a family] —**raised, rais´ing** ◆**n.** a making or becoming larger; especially, an increase in salary or wages

re- *a prefix meaning* **1** again [To *reappear* is to appear again.] **2** back [To *repay* is to pay back.]

read¹ (rēd) **v.** **1** to get the meaning of something written or printed by understanding its letters, signs, or numbers [I *read* the book. She *reads* the gas meter. Can you *read* music?] **2** to speak printed or written words aloud [*Read* the story to me.] —**read** (red), **read´ing**

read² (red) *past tense and past participle of* **read¹** ◆**adj.** having knowledge got from reading; informed [They are both well-*read*.]

read·y (red´ē) **adj.** prepared to act or to be used at once [Is everyone *ready* to leave? Your bath is *ready*.] —**read´i·er, read´i·est** ◆**v.** to prepare [to *ready* the house for guests] —**read´ied, read´y·ing** —**read´i·ness n.**

rea·son (rē′zən) *n.* something said or written to explain an act, idea, or event ◆*v.* **1** to think in a sensible way; come to a conclusion by considering facts **2** to argue in a careful, sensible way

re·build (rē bild′) *v.* to build again, especially something that was damaged, ruined, etc. —**re·built′, re·build′ing**

re·cop·y (rē käp′ē) *v.* to make another copy [*Recopy* the worksheet.] —**re·cop′ied, re·cop′ying**

re·de·sign (rē di zīn′) *v.* to rethink and draw plans for again

re·group (rē grōōp′) *v.* to gather into a group again

re·load (rē lōd′) *v.* to load again [They *reloaded* the boxes into the truck.]

re·mind (rē mīnd′) *v.* to make remember or think of [*Remind* me to pay the gas bill.]

re·name (rē nām′) *v.* to give a new or different name to [Ceylon was *renamed* Sri Lanka.] —**re·named′, re·nam′ing**

re·pair (ri per′) *v.* to fix or mend [He *repaired* the broken toy.]

re·place (rē plās′) *v.* **1** to put back in the right place [*Replace* the tools on my bench when you are through.] **2** to take the place of [Many workers have been *replaced* by computers.] **3** to put another in the place of one used, lost, broken, etc. [to *replace* a worn tire] —**re·placed′, re·plac′ing**

re·ply (rē plī′) *v.* to answer by saying or doing something [to *reply* to a question; to *reply* to the enemy's fire with a counterattack] —**re·plied′, re·ply′ing** ◆*n.* an answer. —*pl.* **re·plies′**

re·think (rē thiŋk′) *v.* to think about again; reconsider —**re·thought′, re·think′ing**

re·write (rē rīt′) *v.* to write again or in different words; revise [to *rewrite* a story] —**re·wrote′, re·writ′ten, re·writ′ing**

rich (rich) *adj.* **1** having wealth; owning much money or property; wealthy **2** having much of something; well supplied [Tomatoes are *rich* in vitamin C.] **3** full of fats, or fats and sugar [*rich* foods] —**rich′ly** *adv.* —**rich′ness** *n.*

rise (rīz) *v.* **1** to stand up or get up from a lying or sitting position **2** to become greater, higher, or stronger [The temperature *rose*. Prices are *rising*. Her voice *rose*.] —**rose, ris′en, ris′ing** ◆*n.* **1** a piece of ground higher than that around it [There's a good view of the countryside from the top of the *rise*.] **2** the fact of becoming greater, higher, etc.; increase [a *rise* in prices]

rock[1] (räk) *n.* a large mass of stone

rock[2] (räk) *v.* to move or swing back and forth or from side to side [to *rock* a cradle] ◆*n.* a rocking movement

roof (rōōf *or* rŏŏf) *n.* **1** the outside top covering of a building **2** anything like a roof in the way it is placed or used [the *roof* of the mouth; the *roof* of a car] —**roof′less** *adj.*

rough (ruf) *adj.* **1** not smooth or level; uneven [a *rough* road; *rough* fur] **2** full of noise and wild action; disorderly [*rough* play] **3** not gentle or mild, as in manners; rude, harsh, etc. [*rough* language] **4** having little comfort or luxury [the *rough* life of a pioneer]

round (round) *adj.* shaped like a ball, a circle, or a tube; having an outline that forms a circle or curve [The world is *round*. Wheels are *round*. The ship has a *round* smokestack.] ◆*n.* a short song for two or more persons or groups, in which the second starts when the first gets to the second phrase, and so on

rush (rush) *v.* **1** to move, send, take, etc., with great speed [I *rushed* from the room. We *rushed* him to a hospital.] **2** to act in haste, without thinking carefully [Don't *rush* into marriage.] ◆*adj.* that must be done or sent in a hurry [a *rush* order]

a	ask, fat
ā	ape, date
ä	car, lot
e	elf, ten
ē	even, meet
i	is, hit
ī	ice, fire
ō	open, go
ô	law, horn
oi	oil, point
o͝o	look, pull
o͞o	ooze, tool
ou	out, crowd
u	up, cut
ʉ	fur, fern
ə	a in ago
	e in agent
	e in father
	i in unity
	o in collect
	u in focus
ch	chin, arch
ŋ	ring, singer
sh	she, dash
th	thin, truth
th	then, father
zh	s in pleasure

Ss

safe (sāf) *adj.* free from harm or danger —**saf´er, saf´est** ◆*n.* a strong metal box with a lock, in which to keep money or valuables

said (sed) *past tense and past participle of* **say** ◆*adj.* named or mentioned before [The *said* contract is no longer in force.]

sail (sāl) *n.* **1** a sheet of heavy cloth such as canvas, used on a ship or boat to move it by catching the wind **2** a trip in a ship or boat, especially one moved by sails [Let's go for a *sail*.] ◆*v.* **1** to travel on water [This liner *sails* between Miami and New York.] **2** to move smoothly [a hawk *sailing* in the sky]

sale (sāl) *n.* **1** the act of selling or exchanging something for money [The clerk made ten *sales* today.] **2** a special selling of goods at prices lower than usual [a clearance *sale*]

sat·is·fy (sat´is fī´) *v.* to meet the needs or wishes of; to content; to please [Only first prize will *satisfy* him.] —**sat´is·fied´, sat´is·fy´ing**

Sat·ur·day (sat´ər dā) *n.* the seventh and last day of the week

sau·sage (sô´sij *or* sä´sij) *n.* pork or other meat, chopped up and seasoned and, usually, stuffed into a tube made of thin skin

scarf (skärf) *n.* a long or broad piece of cloth worn about the head, neck, or shoulders for warmth or decoration —*pl.* **scarves** (skärvz) or **scarfs**

scent (sent) *n.* **1** a smell; odor [the *scent* of apple blossoms] **2** the sense of smell [Lions hunt partly by *scent*.]

school[1] (sko͞ol) *n.* **1** a place, usually a special building, for teaching and learning, as a public school, dancing school, college, etc. **2** the students and teachers of a school [an assembly for the *school*] ◆*adj.* of or for a school or schools [our *school* band]

school[2] (sko͞ol) *n.* a large group of fish or water animals of the same kind swimming together [a *school* of porpoises] ◆*v.* to swim together in a school

scold (skōld) *v.* to find fault with someone in an angry way [I *scolded* her for being late.]

scoop (sko͞op) *n.* **1** a kitchen tool like a small shovel, used to take up sugar, flour, etc., or one with a small, round bowl for dishing up ice cream, etc. **2** the amount taken up at one time by a scoop [three *scoops* of ice cream] ◆*v.* to take up as with a scoop [We *scooped* it up with our hands.]

scram·ble (skram´bəl) *v.* to cook eggs while stirring the mixed whites and yolks —**scram´bled, scram´bling**

scratch (skrach) *v.* **1** to mark or cut the surface of slightly with something sharp [Thorns *scratched* her legs. Our cat *scratched* the chair with its claws.] **2** to rub or scrape, as with the nails, to relieve itching [to *scratch* a mosquito bite] **3** to cross out by drawing lines through [She *scratched* out what he had written.] ◆*n.* **1** a mark or cut made in a surface by something sharp **2** a slight wound **3** a harsh, grating sound [the *scratch* of chalk on a chalkboard]

scream (skrēm) *v.* to give a loud, shrill cry, as in fright or pain [They *screamed* as the roller coaster hurtled downward.] ◆*n.* a loud, shrill cry or sound; shriek

screen (skrēn) *n.* **1** a mesh woven loosely of wires so as to leave small openings between them: screens are used in windows, doors, etc., to keep insects out **2** a covered frame or curtain used to hide, separate, or protect **3** a surface on which movies, television pictures, etc., are shown

sea·shore (sē´shôr) *n.* land by the sea

sea·son (sē´zən) *n.* one of the four parts into which the year is divided: winter, spring, summer, or fall

seat (sēt) *n.* **1** a thing to sit on, as a chair, bench, etc. **2** a place to sit or the right to sit [to buy two *seats* for the opera; to win a *seat* in the Senate] ◆*v.* **1** to cause to sit; put in or on a seat [*Seat* yourself quickly.] **2** to have seats for [This car *seats* six people.]

see (sē) *v.* **1** to be aware of through the eyes; have or use the sense of sight [We *saw* two birds. I don't *see* so well.] **2** to get the meaning of; understand [Do you *see* the point of the joke?] **3** to visit with [We stopped to *see* a friend.] **4** to go to for information or advice; consult [*See* a doctor about your cough.] **5** to think or try to remember [Let me *see*, where did I put that?] —**saw, seen, see´ing**

seek (sēk) *v.* to try to find; search for [to *seek* gold] —**sought, seek´ing**

seen (sēn) *past participle of* **see**

sel·fish (sel´fish) *adj.* caring too much about oneself, with little or no thought or care for others —**self´ish·ly** *adv.* —**self´ish·ness** *n.*

send (send) *v.* **1** to cause to be carried [Food was *sent* by plane.] **2** to cause a message to be transmitted by mail, radio, or other means [I will *send* the letter tomorrow.] **3** to cause or force to go [The teacher *sent* her home.] —**sent, send´ing**

sent (sent) *past tense and past participle of* **send**

serve (surv) *v.* **1** to aid; to help [She *served* her country well.] **2** to wait on [The waiter *served* our table first.] —**served, serv´ing**

ser·vice (sur´vis) *n.* **1** work done for others [Our janitor performs many *services* each day.] **2** a way of providing people with something [We have good telephone *service* in town.] ◆*v.* to repair or adjust [They *service* radios and CD players.] —**ser´viced, ser´vic·ing**

set (set) *v.* **1** to put in a certain place or position [*Set* the book on the table.] **2** to put in order or in the right condition, position, etc.; arrange; adjust [to *set* a trap; to *set* a

thermostat; to *set* a broken bone; to *set* a table for a meal] **3** to establish or fix, as a time for a meeting, a price, a rule, a limit, etc. **4** to sink below the horizon [The sun *sets* in the west.] —**set, set´ting** ◆*n.* **1** a number of parts put together, as in a cabinet [a TV *set*] **2** in mathematics, any collection of units, points, numbers, etc.

set·ting (set´iŋ) *n.* the time, place, and circumstances of an event, story, play, etc.

shad·ow (shad´ō) *n.* the darkness or the dark shape cast upon a surface by something cutting off light from it [Her large hat put her face in *shadow*. His hand cast a *shadow* on the wall.]

shape (shāp) *n.* the way a thing looks because of its outline; outer form; figure [The cloud had the *shape* of a lamb.] ◆*v.* to give a certain shape to; form [The potter *shaped* the clay into a bowl.] —**shaped, shap´ing**

share (sher) *n.* a part that each one of a group gets or has [your *share* of the cake; my *share* of the blame] ◆*v.* to have a share of with others; have or use together [The three of you will *share* the back seat.] —**shared, shar´ing**

sharp (shärp) *adj.* **1** having a thin edge for cutting or a fine point for piercing [a *sharp* knife; a *sharp* needle] **2** very clever or shrewd [a *sharp* mind] ◆*adv.* exactly or promptly [She gets up at 6:30 *sharp*.] —**sharp´ly** *adv.* —**sharp´ness** *n.*

sheep (shēp) *n.* an animal that chews its cud and is related to the goat: its body is covered with heavy wool, and its flesh is used as food, called mutton —*pl.* **sheep**

shelf (shelf) *n.* a thin, flat length of wood, metal, etc., fastened against a wall or built into a frame so as to hold things [the top *shelf* of a bookcase] —*pl.* **shelves**

shelves (shelvz) *n.* *plural of* **shelf**

a	ask, fat
ā	ape, date
ä	car, lot
e	elf, ten
ē	even, meet
i	is, hit
ī	ice, fire
ō	open, go
ô	law, horn
σi	oil, point
σʊ	look, pull
o͞o	ooze, tool
ou	out, crowd
u	up, cut
ʉ	fur, fern
ə	a in ago
	e in agent
	e in father
	i in unity
	o in collect
	u in focus
ch	chin, arch
ŋ	ring, singer
sh	she, dash
th	thin, truth
th	then, father
zh	s in pleasure

177

shine (shīn) **v.** **1** to give off light or reflect light; be bright [The sun *shines*. Her hair *shone*.] **2** to make bright by polishing [to *shine* shoes] —**shone** or **shined, shin´ing** ◆**n.** the act of polishing, as shoes

ship (ship) **n.** a vessel, larger than a boat, for traveling on deep water ◆**v.** to take or send in a ship or by some other means of transport [The cargo was *shipped* from New York.] —**shipped, ship´ping**

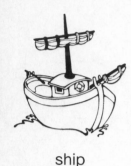

ship

shirt (shʉrt) **n.** **1** the common garment worn by a boy or man on the upper part of the body

shi·ver (shiv´ər) **v.** to shake or tremble, often from fear or cold [We *shivered* when we heard scary sounds.]

shoot (shoot) **v.** to send a bullet, arrow, etc., from [to *shoot* a gun] —**shot, shoot´ing** ◆**n.** a new growth; sprout —**shoot´er n.**

short (shôrt) **adj.** **1** not measuring much from end to end or from beginning to end; not long [a *short* stick; a *short* trip; a *short* novel; a *short* wait] **2** not tall; low [a *short* tree] **3** less or having less than what is enough or correct [Our supply of food is *short*. We are *short* ten dollars.] **4** taking a shorter time to say than other sounds [The "e" in "bed" and the "i" in "rib" are *short*.] ◆**adv.** so as to be short [Cut your speech *short*. We fell *short* of our goal.] ◆**v.** to give less than what is needed, usual, etc. [The cashier *shorted* the customer a dollar.]

shoul·der (shōl´dər) **n.** the part of the body to which an arm or foreleg is connected

should·n't (shood´nt) **contraction** should not

shov·el (shuv´əl) **n.** a tool with a broad scoop and a handle, for lifting and moving loose material ◆**v.** to lift and move with a shovel [to *shovel* coal] —**shov´eled** or **shov´elled, shov´el·ing** or **shov´el·ling**

shy (shī) **adj.** **1** easily frightened; timid [a *shy* animal] **2** not at ease with other people; bashful [a *shy* child] —**shy´er** or **shi´er, shy´est** or **shi´est** —**shy´ly adv.** —**shy´ness n.**

side·walk (sīd´wôk) **n.** a path for walking; usually paved, along the side of a street

sigh (sī) **v.** to let out a long, deep, sounded breath, usually to show that one is sad, tired, relieved, etc. ◆**n.** the act or sound of sighing [She breathed a *sigh* of relief.]

sight (sīt) **n.** **1** something that is seen; especially, something unusual worth seeing [The Grand Canyon is a *sight* you won't forget.] **2** the ability to see; vision; eyesight [He lost his *sight* in the war.] **3** the distance over which one can see [The airplane passed out of *sight*.] ◆**v.** to see [The sailor *sighted* land.]

sign (sīn) **n.** **1** a thing or act that stands for something else; symbol [Black is worn as a *sign* of grief. She saluted the flag as a *sign* of respect. The *sign* (+) means "add."] **2** a board, card, etc., put up in a public place, with information, a warning, etc., on it [The *sign* said, "Do not enter."] **3** anything that tells of the existence or coming of something else [Red spots on the face may be a *sign* of measles.] ◆**v.** to write one's name on [to *sign* a contract to make it legal]

since (sins) **adv.** from then until now [Lynn came Monday and has been here ever *since*.] ◆**prep.** from or during the time given until now [I've been up *since* dawn.] ◆**conj.** **1** after the time that [It's been two years *since* I saw you.] **2** because [You may have these tools, *since* I no longer need them.]

sis·ter (sis´tər) **n.** a girl or woman as she is related to the other children of her parents

sixth (siksth) **adj.** coming after five others; 6th in order ◆**n.** one of the six equal parts of something; 1/6

six·ty (siks´tē) **n.** the cardinal number that is equal to six times ten; 60 —*pl.* **six´ties**

size (sīz) *n.* **1** the amount of space taken up by a thing; how large or how small a thing is [Tell me the *size* of your room. He is strong for his *size*.] **2** any of a series of measures, often numbered, for grading things [She wears a *size* 12 dress.] ◆*v.* to arrange according to size —**sized, siz´ing**

skate (skāt) *n.* a shoe with a metal blade or wheels for gliding across the ice or smooth ground ◆*v.* to move along on skates —**skat´ed, skat´ing**

skim (skim) *v.* **1** to take off floating matter from the top of a liquid [She *skimmed* the milk.] **2** to read quickly [Mary *skimmed* over the newspaper.] **3** to glide lightly over [The dragonfly *skimmed* over the pond.] —**skimmed, skim´ming**

slight (slīt) *adj.* small in amount or degree; not great, strong, important, etc. [a *slight* change in temperature; a *slight* advantage; a *slight* bruise] —**slight´ ly** *adv.*

slip (slip) *v.* **1** to go or pass quietly or without being noticed; escape [We *slipped* out the door. It *slipped* my mind. Time *slipped* by.] **2** to move, shift, or drop, as by accident [The plate *slipped* from my hand.] **3** to slide by accident [He *slipped* on the ice.] —**slipped, slip´ping**

slum·ber (slum´bər) *v.* **1** to sleep **2** to be quiet or inactive [The volcano has *slumbered* for years.] ◆*n.* sleep

sly (slī) *adj.* able to fool or trick others; cunning; crafty [the *sly* fox] —**sli´ er** or **sly´er, sli´ est** or **sly´est** —**sly´ ly** *adv.*

smart (smärt) *adj.* **1** intelligent or clever [a *smart* student] **2** neat, clean, and well-groomed **3** of the newest fashion; stylish [a *smart* new hat] ◆*v.* to cause a sharp, stinging pain [A bee sting *smarts*.] —**smart´ ly** *adv.* —**smart´ ness** *n.*

smile (smīl) *v.* to show that one is pleased, happy, amused, etc., or sarcastic or scornful, by making the corners of the mouth turn up —**smiled, smil´ ing** ◆*n.* the act of smiling or the look on one's face when one smiles

smog·gy (smôg´ē *or* smäg´ē) *adj.* full of polluted air —**smog´gi·er, smog´gi·est**

soak (sōk) *v.* **1** to make or become completely wet by keeping or staying in a liquid [She *soaked* her sore hand in hot water. Let the beans *soak* overnight to soften them.] **2** to suck up or absorb [Use a sponge to *soak* up that water.] ◆*n.* the act of soaking

some (sum) *adj.* **1** being a certain one or ones not named or not known [*Some* people were playing ball.] **2** being of a certain but not a definite number or amount [Have *some* candy.] ◆*pron.* a certain number or amount, but not all [Take *some*.]

somewhat (sum´hwut *or* sum´wut) *adv.* to some degree; rather; a little [They are *somewhat* late.]

soon (soon) *adv.* **1** in a short time; before much time has passed [Spring will *soon* be here.] **2** fast or quickly [as *soon* as possible] **3** ahead of time; early [She left too *soon*.]

soot (soot) *n.* a black powder formed when some things burn: it is mostly carbon and makes smoke gray or black

soothe (sooth) *v.* **1** to make quiet or calm by being gentle or friendly [The clerk *soothed* the angry customer with helpful answers.] **2** to take away some of the pain or sorrow of; ease [I hope this lotion will *soothe* your sunburn.] —**soothed, sooth´ ing** —**sooth´ ing· ly** *adv.*

sought (sôt *or* sät) *past tense and past participle of* **seek**

spare (sper) *v.* to save or free from something [*Spare* us from listening to that story again.] ◆*adj.* kept for use when needed [a *spare* tire]

speak (spēk) *v.* **1** to say something with the voice; talk [They *spoke* to each other on the phone.] **2** to make a speech [Who *speaks* first on the show?]

a	ask, fat
ā	ape, date
ä	car, lot
e	elf, ten
ē	even, meet
i	is, hit
ī	ice, fire
ō	open, go
ô	law, horn
oi	oil, point
oo	look, pull
oo	ooze, tool
ou	out, crowd
u	up, cut
ʉ	fur, fern
ə	a in ago
	e in agent
	e in father
	i in unity
	o in collect
	u in focus
ch	chin, arch
ŋ	ring, singer
sh	she, dash
th	thin, truth
th	then, father
zh	s in pleasure

spill

spe·cial (spesh'əl) *adj.* **1** not like others; different; distinctive [The cook has a *special* recipe for tacos.] **2** unusual; extraordinary [Your idea has *special* merit.] **3** more than others; chief; main [her *special* friend] —**spe´cial·ly** *adv.*

speed·y (spēd'ē) *adj.* very fast [*speedy* runners] —**speed´i·er, speed´i·est** —**speed´i·ly** *adv.* —**speed´i·ness** *n.*

spend (spend) *v.* to pay out or give up, as money, time, or effort [He *spent* $50 for food. *Spend* some time with me.] —**spent, spend´ing** —**spend´er** *n.*

spied (spīd) *past tense and past participle of* **spy**

spill (spil) *v.* to let flow over or run out [Who *spilled* water on the floor? Try not to *spill* any sugar.] —**spilled** or **spilt, spill´ing** ◆*n.* **1** the act of spilling. **2** a fall or tumble, as from a horse: *used only in everyday talk*

splash (splash) *v.* **1** to make a liquid scatter and fall in drops [to *splash* water or mud about] **2** to dash a liquid on, so as to wet or soil [The car *splashed* my coat.] —**splash´y** *adj.*

split (split) *v.* to separate or divide along the length into two or more parts [to *split* an apple] —**split, split´ting** ◆*n.* a break, crack, or tear [a *split* in the seam of a dress] ◆*adj.* broken into parts; divided

split·ting (split'iŋ) *adj.* very painful [a *splitting* headache]

spoil (spoil) *v.* **1** to make or become useless, worthless, or rotten; to damage; to ruin [Ink stains *spoiled* the paper.] **2** to cause a person to ask for or expect too much by giving in to all of that person's wishes [to *spoil* a child] —**spoiled, spoil´ing**

sprang (spraŋ) *past tense of* **spring**

spray (sprā) *n.* a mist of tiny drops, as of water thrown off from a waterfall ◆*v.* to put something on in a spray [to *spray* a car with paint] —**spray´er** *n.*

spread (spred) *v.* **1** to open out or stretch out, in space or time [*Spread* out the tablecloth. The eagle *spread* its wings. Our trip *spread* out over two weeks.] **2** to put or cover in a thin layer [to *spread* bread with jelly] ◆*n.* **1** a cloth cover, as for a table or bed **2** any soft substance, as jam or butter, that can be spread in a layer —**spread´er** *n.*

spring (spriŋ) *v.* **1** to move suddenly and quickly; leap; jump up [I *sprang* to my feet.] **2** to snap back into position or shape, as a rubber band that is stretched and then let go —**sprang** or **sprung, sprung, spring´ing** ◆*n.* **1** a device, as a coil of wire, that returns to its original shape when pressure on it is released: used in beds and automobiles to take up shock or in clocks, etc., to make them go **2** water flowing up from the ground **3** the season when plants begin to grow, between winter and summer

spy (spī) *n.* a person who watches others secretly and carefully. —*pl.* **spies** ◆*v.* to watch closely and secretly [She likes to *spy* on her neighbors.] —**spied, spy´ing**

squirm (skwʉrm) *v.* to twist and turn the body as a snake does; wriggle; writhe [The rabbit *squirmed* out of the trap.]

stain (stān) *v.* to spoil with dirt or a patch of color; to soil or spot [The rug was *stained* with ink.] ◆*n.* a dirty or colored spot [grass *stains*]

stand (stand) *v.* **1** to be or get in an upright position on one's feet [*Stand* by your desk.] **2** to be or place in an upright position on its base, bottom, etc. [Our trophy *stands* on the shelf. *Stand* the broom in the corner.] **3** to be placed or situated [Our house *stands* on a hill.] —**stood, stand´ing**

start (stärt) *v.* **1** to begin to go, do, act, be, etc. [We *start* for Toledo today. The show *starts* at 8:30.] **2** to cause to begin; set in motion or action [*Start* the car. Who *started* the fight?] ◆*n.* the act of starting or beginning

stead·y (sted'ē) *adj.* **1** firm or stable; not shaky [a *steady* chair] **2** not changing or letting up; regular [a *steady* rain] —**stead´i·er, stead´i·est**

steel (stēl) *n.* a hard, tough metal made of iron mixed with a little carbon

stem (stem) *n.* the main part of a plant or tree that grows up from the ground and bears the leaves, flowers, or fruit

step (step) *n.* **1** the act of moving and placing the foot forward, backward, sideways, up, or down, as in walking, dancing, or climbing **2** a place to rest the foot in going up or down, as a stair or the rung of a ladder ◆*v.* to move by taking a step or steps —**stepped, step´ping**

sting (stiŋ) *v.* **1** to hurt by pricking [Wasps can *sting* you.] **2** to cause or feel sharp pain [The cold wind *stung* her cheeks.] —**stung, sting´ing** ◆*n.* the act or power of stinging [The *sting* of a bee may be dangerous.]

stir (stʉr) *v.* to move or shake slightly [Not a leaf *stirred* in the quiet air.] —**stirred, stir´ring**

stone (stōn) *n.* **1** hard mineral matter that is found in the earth but is not metal; rock [a monument built of *stone*] **2** a small piece of this [Don't throw *stones*. Rubies are precious *stones*.]

stood (stʊod) *past tense and past participle of* **stand**

stop (stäp) *v.* **1** to halt or keep from going on, moving, acting, etc.; bring or come to an end [My watch *stopped*. The noise *stopped*. *Stop* the car. They *stopped* us from talking.] **2** to clog or block [The drain in the sink is *stopped* up.] **3** to stay or visit [We *stopped* there overnight.] —**stopped, stop´ping** ◆*n.* **1** a place stopped at [a *stop* on a bus route] **2** the act or fact of stopping; finish; end [Put a *stop* to this argument.]

stran·ger (strān´jər) *n.* **1** a person who is new to a place; outsider or foreigner **2** a person not known to one [Don't speak to *strangers*.]

straw·ber·ry (strô´ber´ē) *n.* the small, red, juicy fruit of a low plant of the rose family —*pl.* **straw´ber´ries**

stream (strēm) *n.* a flow of water; especially, a small river ◆*v.* **1** to flow in a stream **2** to pour out or flow [eyes *streaming* with tears]

street (strēt) *n.* a road in a city or town; also, such a road with its sidewalks and buildings

strike (strīk) *v.* **1** to hit by giving a blow, coming against with force, etc. [Nina *struck* him in anger. The car *struck* the curb.] **2** to make a sound by hitting some part [The clock *struck* one. *Strike* middle C on the piano.] **3** to set on fire as by rubbing [to *strike* a match] **4** to stop working until certain demands have been met [The workers are *striking* for shorter hours.] —**struck, struck** or **strick´en, strik´ing**

string (striŋ) *n.* **1** a thick thread or thin strip of cloth, leather, etc., used for tying or pulling; cord **2** a number of things in a row [a *string* of lights] ◆*v.* **1** to put on a string [to *string* beads] **2** to stretch like a string; extend [to *string* telephone wires on poles; to *string* out a speech] —**strung, string´ing**

strong (strôŋ) *adj.* **1** having great force or power; not weak; powerful [a *strong* person; *strong* winds] **2** having a powerful effect on the senses or mind; not mild [a *strong* taste, smell, light, sound, liking, etc.] —**strong´ly** *adv.* —**strong´ness** *n.*

struck (struk) *past tense and a past participle of* **strike**

stud·y (stud´ē) *v.* **1** to try to learn by reading, thinking, etc. [to *study* law] **2** to look at or into carefully; examine or investigate [We must *study* the problem of crime.] **3** to read so as to understand and remember [to *study* a lesson] —**stud´ied, stud´y·ing** ◆*n.* **1** a branch of learning; subject [the *study* of medicine] **2** a room used for studying, reading, etc. —*pl.* **stud´ies**

sug·ar (sʰʊog´ər) *n.* any of certain sweet substances in the form of crystals that dissolve in water: glucose, lactose, and sucrose are different kinds of sugar; sucrose is the common sugar used to sweeten food

a	ask, fat
ā	ape, date
ä	car, lot
e	elf, ten
ē	even, meet
i	is, hit
ī	ice, fire
ō	open, go
ô	law, horn
σi	oil, point
σo	look, pull
ōō	ooze, tool
ou	out, crowd
u	up, cut
ʉ	fur, fern
ə	a in ago
	e in agent
	e in father
	i in unity
	o in collect
	u in focus
ch	chin, arch
ŋ	ring, singer
sh	she, dash
th	thin, truth
th	then, father
zh	s in pleasure

181

swim

sur·prise (sər prīz′) *v.* to cause to feel wonder by being unexpected [Her sudden anger *surprised* us.] —**sur·prised′, sur·pris′ing** ◆*n.* the act of surprising [The news took them by *surprise*.]

sway (swā) *v.* to swing or bend back and forth or from side to side [The flowers *swayed* in the breeze.] —**swayed, sway′ing**

sweat·er (swet′ər) *n.* a knitted outer garment for the upper part of the body

swim (swim) *v.* to move in water by working the arms, legs, fins, etc. —**swam, swum, swim′ming** ◆*n.* an act, time, or distance of swimming —**swim′mer** *n.*

Tt

take (tāk) *v.* **1** to get hold of; grasp [*Take* my hand as we cross the street.] **2** to write down; copy [*Take* notes on the lecture.] **3** to carry [*Take* your skis with you.] **4** to lead or bring [Ti *took* Lee to the movie. This road *takes* us to the park.] —**took, tak′en, tak′ing**

tale (tāl) *n.* a story about things that are made up or imagined [a fairy *tale*]

tar·dy (tär′dē) *adj.* not on time; late [I was *tardy* for my class.] —**tard′i·er, tard′i·est** —**tar′di·ly** *adv.* —**tar′di·ness** *n.*

tax (taks) *n.* money that one must pay to help support a government: it is usually a percentage of one's income or of the value of something bought or owned —*pl.* **tax′es** —**tax′a·ble** *adj.*

teach·er (tēch′ər) *n.* a person who teaches, especially in a school or college

team (tēm) *n.* **1** two or more horses, oxen, etc., harnessed together as for pulling a plow or wagon **2** a group of people working together or playing together in a contest against another such group [a *team* of scientists; a baseball *team*] ◆*v.* to join together in a team [Let's *team* up with them.]

teeth (tēth) *n.* *plural of* **tooth**

ten·der (ten′dər) *adj.* **1** soft or delicate and easily chewed or cut [a *tender* piece of meat] **2** feeling pain or hurting easily; sensitive [My sprained ankle still feels *tender*.] **3** warm and gentle; loving [a *tender* smile]

than (than *or* thən) *conj.* compared to: *than* is used before the second part of a comparison [I am taller *than* you.]

thank (thaŋk) *v.* to say that one is grateful to another for a kindness [We *thanked* her for her help.]

that (that *or* thət) *pron.* **1** the person or thing mentioned [*That* is José.] **2** who, whom, or which [She's the one *that* I saw. Here's the book *that* I borrowed.] —*pl.* **those**

that's (thats *or* thəts) *contraction* that is

thaw (thô) *v.* **1** to melt [The snow *thawed*.] **2** to become unfrozen: said of frozen foods ◆*n.* weather that is warm enough to melt snow and ice

them (them) *pron.* the form of **they** that is used as the object of a verb or preposition [I met *them* at the airport. Give the flowers to *them*.]

there's (therz) *contraction* there is

they'll (thāl) *contraction* **1** they will **2** they shall

they're (ther) *contraction* they are

thief (thēf) *n.* a person who steals, especially one who steals secretly —*pl.* **thieves** (thēvz)

think (thiŋk) *v.* **1** to use the mind; reason [*Think* before you act.] **2** to form or have in the mind [She was *thinking* happy thoughts.] —**thought, think′ing**

third (thurd) *adj.* coming after two others; 3rd in order ◆*n.* one of three equal parts of something; 1/3

thir·teen (thur′tēn′) *n., adj.* three more than ten; the number 13

thir·ty (thurt′ē) *n., adj.* three times ten; the number 30 —*pl.* **thir′ties**

thought¹ (thôt) *n.* **1** the act or process of thinking [When deep in *thought*, he doesn't hear.] **2** what one thinks; idea, opinion, plan, etc. [a penny for your *thoughts*]

thought² (thôt) *past tense and past participle of* **think**

thread (thred) *n.* a very thin cord used in sewing and made of strands of spun cotton, silk, etc., twisted together ►*v.* to put a thread through the eye of [to *thread* a needle] —**thread´like** *adj.*

thrill (thril) *v.* to feel or make greatly excited; shiver or tingle with strong feeling [She *thrilled* at the praise. That movie *thrilled* us.] ►*n.* a strong feeling of excitement that makes one shiver [Seeing a lion gave me a *thrill*.]

throat (thrōt) *n.* 1 the front part of the neck 2 the upper part of the passage from the mouth to the stomach or lungs [I have a sore *throat*.]

throne (thrōn) *n.* the raised chair on which a king or other important person sits during ceremonies

through (thrō̅o̅) *prep.* 1 in one side and out the other side of; from end to end of [The nail went *through* the board. We drove *through* the tunnel.] 2 from the beginning to the end of [We stayed in Maine *through* the summer.] ►*adv.* in a complete and thorough way; entirely [We were soaked *through* by the rain.] ►*adj.* finished [Are you *through* with your homework?]

throw (thrō) *v.* to send through the air by a fast motion of the arm; hurl, toss, etc. [to *throw* a ball] —**threw, thrown, throw´ing** ►*n.* the act of throwing [The fast *throw* put the runner out at first base.]

thumb (thum) *n.* the short, thick finger nearest the wrist ►*v.* to handle, turn, soil, etc., with the thumb [to *thumb* the pages of a book]

tide (tīd) *n.* the regular rise and fall of the ocean's surface, about every twelve hours, caused by the attraction of the moon and sun ►*v.* to help in overcoming a time of trouble [Will $10 *tide* you over until Monday?] —**tid´ed, tid´ing**

tie (tī) *v.* 1 to bind together or fasten with string, rope, cord, etc. [They *tied* his hands together. *Tie* the boat to the pier.] 2 to equal, as in a score [Pablo *tied* with Carmela for first place.] —**tied, ty´ing** ►*n.* 1 *a shorter word for* **necktie** 2 the fact of being equal, as in a score; also, a contest in which scores are equal —*pl.* **ties**

to (tō̅o̅ *or* to͝o *or* tə) *prep.* 1 in the direction of [Turn *to* the right.] 2 on, onto, against, etc. [Put your hand *to* your mouth. Apply the lotion *to* the skin.]

too (tō̅o̅) *adv.* 1 in addition; besides; also [You come, *too*.] 2 more than enough [This hat is *too* big.] 3 very [You are *too* kind.]

toss (tôs *or* täs) *v.* to throw from the hand in a light way [to *toss* a ball]

tot·al (tōt´l) *n.* the whole amount; sum ►*adj.* making up the whole amount; entire [The *total* amount of your bill is $10.50.] ►*v.* to find the sum or total of —**to´tal·ly** *adv.*

tough (tuf) *adj.* 1 able to bend or twist without tearing or breaking [*tough* rubber] 2 rough or brutal [Don't get *tough* with me.]

town (toun) *n.* a place where there are a large number of houses and other buildings, larger than a village but smaller than a city

toy (toi) *n.* a thing to play with; especially, a plaything for children ►*adj.* 1 like a toy in size or use [a *toy* dog] 2 made for use as a toy; especially, made as a small model [a *toy* train]

track (trak) *n.* 1 a mark left in passing, as a footprint or wheel rut 2 a path or trail ►*v.* 1 to follow the tracks of [We *tracked* the fox to its den.] 2 to make tracks or dirty marks [The children *tracked* up the clean floor.]

train (trān) *n.* a line of connected railroad cars that is pulled by a locomotive ►*v.* 1 to develop the mind or character 2 to teach or give practice in some skill

trap (trap) *n.* 1 any device for catching animals 2 a trick used to fool or catch someone ►*v.* to catch in a trap —**trapped, trap´ping**

treas·ure (trezh´ər) *n.* 1 money or jewels collected and stored up 2 a person or thing considered valuable ►*v.* 1 to save or store for future use 2 to value greatly —**treas´ured, treas´ur·ing**

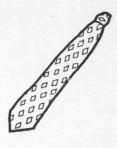

tie

train

a	ask, fat
ā	ape, date
ä	car, lot
e	elf, ten
ē	even, meet
i	is, hit
ī	ice, fire
ō	open, go
ô	law, horn
oi	oil, point
o͝o	look, pull
o̅o̅	ooze, tool
ou	out, crowd
u	up, cut
ʉ	fur, fern
ə	a in ago
	e in agent
	e in father
	i in unity
	o in collect
	u in focus
ch	chin, arch
ŋ	ring, singer
sh	she, dash
th	thin, truth
th	then, father
zh	s in pleasure

183

tried (trīd) *past tense and past participle of* **try**

trim (trim) *v.* to make neat or tidy by cutting or clipping [Becky *trimmed* her hair last night.] —**trimmed, trim′ming**

trip (trip) *v.* to stumble or make stumble [She *tripped* over the rug. Bill put out his foot and *tripped* me.] —**tripped, trip′ping** ◆*n.* a traveling from one place to another and returning; journey, especially a short one

true (trōō) *adj.* agreeing with the facts; not false [a *true* story]

try (trī) *v.* to make an effort; attempt [*Try* to remember the name.] —**tried, try′ing**

tune (tōōn *or* tyōōn) *n.* a series of musical tones with a regular rhythm; melody [She sang a pretty *tune.*]

☆**tur·key** (tur′kē) *n.* **1** a large, wild or tame bird, originally of North America, with a small head and spreading tail **2** its flesh, used as food —*pl.* **tur′keys** or **tur′key**

twen·ty (twen′tē) *n., adj.* two times ten; the number 20 —*pl.* **twen′ties**

two (tōō) *n., adj.* one more than one; the number 2

un- **1** *a prefix meaning* not *or* the opposite of [An *unhappy* person is one who is not happy, but sad.] **2** *a prefix meaning* to reverse *or* undo the action of [To *untie* a shoelace is to reverse the action of tying it.]

un·a·ble (un ā′bəl) *adj.* not able; not having the means or power to do something

un·but·ton (un but′n) *v.* to unfasten the button or buttons of

un·changed (un chānjd′) *adj.* not changed; not different

un·clean (un klēn′) *adj.* dirty; filthy

un·der (un′dər) *prep.* in or to a place, position, amount, value, etc., lower than; below [He sang *under* her window. It rolled *under* the table. It weighs *under* a pound.] ◆*adv.* less in amount, value, etc. [It cost two dollars or *under.*]

un·eas·y (un ē′zē) *adj.* **1** having or giving no ease; not comfortable [an *uneasy* conscience] **2** worried; anxious [Dad felt *uneasy* when I was late.] —**un·eas′i·er, un·eas′i·est**

un·e·ven (un ē′vən) *adj.* not even, level, or smooth; irregular [*uneven* ground] —**un·e′ven·ly adv.** —**un·e′ven·ness n.**

un·load (un lōd′) *v.* to take a load or cargo from a truck, ship, etc.

un·luck·y (un luk′ē) *adj.* having or bringing bad luck; not lucky; unfortunate [There is a superstition that breaking a mirror is *unlucky.*] —**un·luck′i·er, un·luck′i·est** —**un·luck′i·ly adv.**

un·paid (un pād′) *adj.* not receiving pay [an *unpaid* helper]

un·pre·pared (un′prē perd′) *adj.* not prepared or ready [We are still *unprepared* for the visitors.]

un·seen (un sēn′) *adj.* not seen [We remained *unseen* in the bushes.]

un·sure (un shoor′) *adj.* not sure; uncertain

un·touched (un tucht′) *adj.* **1** not touched; not handled **2** not used; not disturbed

un·true (un trōō′) *adj.* **1** not correct; false **2** not faithful or loyal — **un·tru′ly adv.**

un·wrap (un rap′) *v.* to open by taking off the wrapping; also, to become opened in this way —**un·wrapped′, un·wrap′ping**

use (yōōz) *v.* **1** to put or bring into service or action [*Use* the vacuum cleaner on the rugs. What kind of toothpaste do you *use*?] **2** to do away with by using; consume [She *used* up all the soap. Don't *use* up your energy.] —**used, us′ing**

used (yōōzd) *adj.* that has been used; not new; secondhand [*used* cars]

u·su·al (yo͞o′zho͞o əl) *adj.* such as is most often seen, heard, or used; common; normal [the *usual* time] —**u′su·al·ly** *adv.*

Vv

vase (vās *or* vāz) *n.* an open container used for decoration or for holding flowers —*pl.* **vas′es**

ver·y (ver′ē) *adv.* in a high degree; to a great extent; extremely [*very* cold; *very* funny; *very* sad]

Ww

wag·on (wag′ən) *n.* a vehicle with four wheels, especially for carrying heavy loads

☆**wal·let** (wôl′ət *or* wäl′ət) *n.* a thin, flat case for carrying money, cards, etc., in the pocket

was (wuz *or* wäz) *the form of* **be** *showing the past time with singular nouns and with* I, he, she, *or* it

was·n't (wuz′ənt *or* wäz′ənt) *contraction* was not

watch (wäch *or* wôch) *v.* **1** to keep one's sight on; look at [We *watched* the parade.] **2** to take care of; look after; guard [The shepherd *watched* his flock.] ◆*n.* **1** the act of watching or guarding [The dog keeps *watch* over the house.] **2** a device for telling time that is like a clock but small enough to be worn, as on the wrist, or carried in the pocket — *pl.* **watch′es**

wa·ter (wôt′ər) *n.* the colorless liquid that falls as rain, is found in springs, rivers, lakes, and oceans, and forms a large part of the cells of all living things: it is made up of hydrogen and oxygen, with the chemical formula H_2O ◆*v.* **1** to give water to [to *water* a horse] **2** to supply with water, as by sprinkling [to *water* a lawn]

wax (waks) *n.* **1** a yellow substance that bees make and use for building honeycombs; beeswax **2** any substance like this, as paraffin wax is used to make candles, polishes, etc. ◆*v.* to put wax or polish on

weight (wāt) *n.* **1** heaviness, the quality a thing has because of the pull of gravity on it **2** amount of heaviness [What is your *weight*?] **3** any solid mass used for its heaviness [to lift *weights* for exercise; a paper*weight*]

we'll (wēl) *contraction* **1** we shall **2** we will

wet (wet) *adj.* covered or soaked with water or some other liquid [Wipe it off with a *wet* rag.] —**wet′ter, wet′test**

whack (hwak) *v.* to hit or slap with a sharp sound ◆*n.* a blow that makes a sharp sound; also, this sound

whale (hwāl) *n.* a very large mammal that lives in the sea and looks like a fish

wheel (hwēl) *n.* a round disk or frame that turns on an axle fixed at its center [a wagon *wheel*] ◆*v.* to move on wheels or in a vehicle with wheels [to *wheel* a grocery cart]

where's (hwerz *or* werz) *contraction* **1** where is **2** where has

wheth·er (hwe*th*′ər) *conj.* **1** if it is true or likely that [I don't know *whether* I can go.] **2** in either case that [It makes no difference *whether* he comes or not.]

which (hwich) *pron.* what one or what ones of those being talked about or suggested [*Which* will you choose?]

while (hwīl) *n.* a period of time [I waited a short *while*.] ◆*conj.* during the time that [I read a book *while* I waited.]

whine (hwīn *or* wīn) *v.* to make a long, high sound or cry [The injured dog *whined*.] —**whined, whin′ing**

whirl (hwʉrl *or* wʉrl) *v.* to turn rapidly around and around; spin fast [The dancers *whirled* around the room.]

wheel

a	ask, fat
ā	ape, date
ä	car, lot
e	elf, ten
ē	even, meet
i	is, hit
ī	ice, fire
ō	open, go
ô	law, horn
oi	oil, point
o͝o	look, pull
o͞o	ooze, tool
ou	out, crowd
u	up, cut
ʉ	fur, fern
ə	a in ago
	e in agent
	e in father
	i in unity
	o in collect
	u in focus
ch	chin, arch
ŋ	ring, singer
sh	she, dash
th	thin, truth
th	then, father
zh	s in pleasure

whisk (hwisk) *v.* to move, brush, etc., with a quick, sweeping motion [He *whisked* the lint from his coat with a brush.] ◆*n.* **1** a small broom with a short handle, for brushing clothes: *the full name is* **whisk broom 2** a kitchen tool made up of wire loops fixed in a handle, for whipping eggs, etc.

whisper (hwis′pər) *v.* to speak or say in a low, soft voice, especially without vibrating the vocal cords ◆*n.* soft, low tone of voice [to speak in a *whisper*]

who (hoō) *pron.* what person or persons [*Who* helped you?]

whole (hōl) *adj.* **1** not divided or cut up; in one piece [Put *whole* carrots in the stew.] **2** having all its parts, complete [The *whole* opera is on two records.] ◆*n.* the total amount [He saved the *whole* of his allowance.] —**whole′ness** *n.*

wife (wīf) *n.* the woman to whom a man is married; married woman —*pl.* **wives**

win·ner (win′ər) *n.* **1** one that wins **2** a person who seems very likely to win or be successful: *used only in everyday talk*

witch (wich) *n.* a person, now especially a woman, who is believed to have magic power —*pl.* **witch′es**

wives (wīvz) *n. plural of* **wife**

wolf (woolf) *n.* **1** a wild animal that looks like a dog: it kills other animals for food **2** a person who is fierce, cruel, greedy, etc. —*pl.* **wolves**

wolves (woolvz) *n. plural of* **wolf**

wom·an (woom′ən) *n.* **1** an adult, female human being **2** women as a group —*pl.* **wom′en**

wom·en (wim′ən) *n. plural of* **woman**

won't (wōnt) *contraction* will not

wood·en (wood′n) *adj.* made of wood

wool (wool) *n.* **1** the soft, curly hair of sheep or the hair of some other animals, as the goat or llama **2** yarn, cloth, or clothing made from such hair

wore (wôr) *past tense of* **wear**

☆**work·book** (wurk′book) *n.* a book that has questions and exercises to be worked out by students

world (wurld) *n.* **1** the earth [a cruise around the *world*] **2** the whole universe **3** any planet or place thought of as like the earth [Are there other *worlds* in space?] **4** all people [He thinks the *world* is against him.] **5** some part of the world [the Eastern *world*] **6** some period of history [the *world* of Ancient Rome] **7** some special group of people, things, etc. [the business *world*; the plant *world*]

wor·ry (wur′ē) *v.* to be or make troubled in mind; feel or make uneasy or anxious [Don't *worry*. Her absence *worried* us.] —**wor′ried, wor′ry·ing** ◆*n.* a troubled feeling; anxiety; care [sick with *worry*] —*pl.* **wor′ries**

worse (wurs) *adj.* **1** *the comparative of* **bad** *and* **ill 2** more evil, harmful, bad, unpleasant, etc.; less good [an even *worse* crime] **3** in poorer health; more ill [The patient is *worse* today.] ◆*adv.* **1** *the comparative of* **badly** *and* **ill 2** in a worse way [He acted *worse* than ever.]

would (wood) *the past tense of* **will** [He promised that he *would* return.]

would·n't (wood′nt) *contraction* would not

would've (wood′uv) *contraction* would have

wrap (rap) *v.* **1** to wind or fold around something [She *wrapped* a scarf around her head.] **2** to cover in this way [They *wrapped* the baby in a blanket.] **3** to cover with paper, etc. [to *wrap* a present] —**wrapped** or **wrapt** (rapt), **wrap′ping** ◆*n.* an outer covering or outer garment [Put your *wraps* in the closet.]

wreck (rek) *n.* the remains of something that has been destroyed or badly damaged [an old *wreck* stranded on the reef] ◆*v.* to destroy or damage badly; ruin [to *wreck* a car in an accident; to *wreck* one's plans for a picnic]

wren (ren) *n.* a small songbird with a long bill and a stubby tail that tilts up

wrin·kle (riŋ′kəl) **n.** a small or uneven crease or fold [*wrinkles* in a coat] ◆**v.** **1** to make wrinkles in [a brow that is *wrinkled* with care] **2** to form wrinkles [This cloth *wrinkles* easily.] —**wrin′ kled, wrin′ kling**

write (rīt) **v.** **1** to form words, letters, etc., as with a pen or pencil **2** to form the words, letters, etc., of [*Write* your address here.] **3** to be the author or composer of [Dickens *wrote* novels. Mozart *wrote* symphonies.] **4** to fill in or cover with writing [to *write* a check; to *write* ten pages] **5** to send a message in writing; write a letter [*Write* me every week. He *wrote* that he was ill.] —**wrote, writ′ten, writ′ing**

writ·er (rīt′ər) **n.** a person who writes, especially one whose work is writing books, essays, articles, etc.; author

wrong (rôŋ) **adj.** **1** not right, just, or good; unlawful, wicked, or bad [It is *wrong* to steal.] **2** not the one that is true, correct, wanted, etc. [the *wrong* answer] **3** in error; mistaken [He's not *wrong*.] ◆**n.** something wrong; especially, a wicked or unjust act [Does she know right from *wrong*?] ◆**adv.** in a wrong way, direction, etc.; incorrectly [You did it *wrong*.] —**wrong′ ly adv.** —**wrong′ness n.**

wrote (rōt) *past tense of* **write**

Yy

year (yir) **n.** **1** a period of 365 days, or, in a leap year, 366, divided into 12 months and beginning January 1: it is based on the time taken by the earth to go completely around the sun, about 365 1/4 days **2** any period of twelve months starting at any time [She was six *years* old in July.]

yell (yel) **v.** to cry out loudly; scream ◆**n.** **1** a loud shout **2** a cheer by a crowd, usually in rhythm, as at a football game

your (yo͝or) **pron.** of you or done by you: *this possessive form of* **you** *is used before a noun and thought of as an adjective* [*your* book; *your* work]: *see also* **yours**

you're (yo͝or *or* yo͞or) **contraction** you are

yours (yo͝orz) **pron.** the one or the ones that belong to you: *this form of* **your** *is used when it is not followed by a noun* [Is this pen *yours*? *Yours* cost more than ours.]; *yours* is used as a polite closing of a letter, often with *truly, sincerely,* etc.

you've (yo͞ov) **contraction** you have

a	ask, fat
ā	ape, date
ä	car, lot
e	elf, ten
ē	even, meet
i	is, hit
ī	ice, fire
ō	open, go
ô	law, horn
oi	oil, point
o͝o	look, pull
o͞o	ooze, tool
ou	out, crowd
u	up, cut
ʉ	fur, fern
ə	a in ago
	e in agent
	e in father
	i in unity
	o in collect
	u in focus
ch	chin, arch
ŋ	ring, singer
sh	she, dash
th	thin, truth
th	then, father
zh	s in pleasure

Spelling Notebook

Spelling Notebook

Spelling Notebook

Spelling Notebook

Spelling Notebook